MAH

I could find the words for a million stories
but for you I struggle to find the words
to tell you how much I love and appreciate you.
Every time I go on a search to explain your worth
I end up drenched in tears.
Especially when I look back over the years,
you've paid the price with every sacrifice
that's afforded me comfort in this lifetime.
We didn't always have everything we wanted,
but I had everything I needed.
I'm so sorry for not understanding earlier,
I'm so sorry for not appreciating you more.
You were there for me in ways I didn't understand.
Thank you so much for never giving up on me
when I gave up on me countless times.
Thank you for never leaving me
when I wanted to walk away from
everything countless times.
Thank you for loving me,
believing in me, supporting me, protecting me,
sacrificing for me and praying for me
continuously, unconditionally and abundantly.
Thank you for the days and nights you spent
away from the house working so I would be comfortable,
thank you for days you weren't at your best
but still provided more than your best for me.
Thank you for the times you chose my comfort over yours,
the moments you knew I was being selfish and naive
and still gave me the right of way!
I thank you so much for trusting me in my failures
and loving me no less through them.
You are and have been the closest to God
in how ungrateful I would be naming the ways
you've been being a blessing to me.
I thank the Divine Creator for you and your purpose,
because you've chosen to love me on purpose.
I love you, I regard you,
and I appreciate every single thing about you!
I love you and I am immensely grateful
that time has allowed me
to show my appreciation and love for you!

DEAR MAH,
THANK YOU FOR ALWAYS HAVING MY BACK,
EVEN IF IT MEANT GIVING ME YOURS ...

A GRATEFUL SON.

The Heartbreak Masterpiece

A RAZED UTOPIA

$$\frac{^{5}ChL^{8} \times (R.G)^{5} \times (G^{4}M^{4}S^{4})^{13}}{TGO^{50} \times SGH^{50} \times \infty^{58}} = Alqhumy$$

ALCHEMY

Unsullied- They Told Me

Between clogged pipe dreams
and poorly funded rich schemes.
they told me, if I set my mind to anything,
everything is possible to achieve...
very naive, I believed and fell in line
with the mindless machines in a crippled regime,
that moved to the same repulsive beat drenched in monotony
they preached monotonous obedience on repeat.
Listen as loud booms loom, each boom
signifying the carbon copies of our shared gloom
oh the bondage of being free,
when you're face to face with your life
and don't recognize
you're an echo of an artificial heartbeat?

My friends- listen please!

because they told me there was spice
in the monotony and dull cadence
the drill sergeants ensure drummers
drum to a snail's pace,
as though teaching their drumsticks patience.
But lo I'm no patient,
and I will not be altered nor doctored
between red and blue pills,
nor will I be subjected to common frills
and enslave my individualistic will
just to be subpar, as all the other conformists are.

simply because in me a different sound is drowned...

loud nevertheless drowned
by the multiplicity of conformity
anonymity is the new identity
don't you see how we march
mindlessly in symmetry
and never do we cross the predetermined lines
though blatant still imaginary....
the mind control is legendary
imbibed and hereditary- I was special
'til they beat me to death with ordinary

See they told me, I was never enough and I believed,
I thought being a part of a family was all I'd need.
I forgot myself, traded my heartbeat for wallstreet
they told me that I could be anybody
somebody, in a world resembling nobodies
who knew someone who was capable of being a nobody.

They told me, unending lies,
ignored my persistent whys
I was a puppet with Pinocchio's nose,
denying the truth because
he who knows the nose knew better
but that's how the life of a puppet goes...
I'm strung up, apparently with no hope,
as they deduce my worth,
and seduce me with provocative words

they told me anything
and with everything I believed
very naïve I fell in line with the mindless machines
in a crippled regime- whose ultimate goal
was to bury me leagues beneath the ordinary
and unfortunately they believed
they were the end of me
'til they... saw me...
blossoming through the concrete.

Cuz who cares what they said.

Coffins of Comfort (Tradition)

can you tell me
who told you the sky was closed
or that there was a dead end to hope?
Who told you that this was all you were meant to be,
an apple who would never roll too far from its heredity?
Why did you believe potential had ceilings
and time was swiftly fleeting?
Who told you the legacy you'd inherit was hardships or disease?
When did you accept the death of a genetic defect?
When did failures become family heirlooms
worn boldly as albatrosses of consent?
Who was it that taught you the ease of self-betrayal,
or to be sacrificial lambs of your dreams?
How did you learn to deviate from your successes
in lieu of someone other than you?
Who taught you to juggle the trauma of generational
catastrophes and shortcomings?
Who told you that you should only use your claws
to impede the movement of someone
who shares the same hue as you?
Who was it? Because you should be ashamed
at how you've been constrained to aid in your decay.
Look how far you've been led astray
taught the inaccuracy that destiny should only be a fantasy.

Who taught you
the routine of self-demise where you practice
the destruction of your future before it's ever realized?
Who coaxed you to ignore the brilliance you yield?
How many times have ideas so fresh
been history before they became real?
Who told you because your ancestors suffered
that you should, too?
When were you told that your dreams and aspirations
should be as dark as your hue?
Why? How could you be duped by these lies,
pulling the wool over your own eyes;
adding to the unbankable currency of History's cemetery?
Why did they gift you those subtle crutches
guised as possibilities?
The gall to lie to greatness, the artistry of flummery
where you've been lost in its subtleties.
You are the correction of the ancients—the chosen one of chosen ones.
Step forth, bold and free. Chin up; embrace your inner you.
This life you live is your legacy.
Get out of your own way and let it be.

Ecfundo

Who cares and so what?
Who cares about the millions of others out there?
Who cares about the thousands of failed stories?
Who cares that you're not as popular or as known?
Will you let your version of your talent be cast aside
simply because you want to compete with household names?
Why are you competing with your talents, you giftings,
if it will make room for you?
If your giftings make space for you,
nowhere is too congested, nowhere is too packed,
nowhere is too full where you wouldn't flourish
and be more successful than you could've imagined.
Why are you building doors on your runways of success?
Why are you building cul-de-sacs on your highways?
Why are you stifling yourself of pleasure while dying to live?
You're choking yourself, and asking why you can't breathe?
How many second chances are you going to waste on people
who robbed you the first chance they got?
How many times are you going to give away to the world
items that were only meant for you?
How many times have you squandered your invaluables
or traded them for tears and regrets?
How often will you sacrifice your good nature
because you've been duped by the potential of another?
How many more times will you have the wool
pulled over your eyes while you constantly relive your demise
while feeling lesser and lesser on the inside.
Look at the accumulation of burdens you've been building!
Look at the subtle ways you've been bullying and sabotaging YOUR destiny!
How could you be so blind, deaf, and dumb?
wake up for once and trust yourself
the way you JesusChristed every Judas you ever forgave.
Wake up and for real and get up for you
the way you've Lazarused from the Brutus Blade.
You're choosing to die miserably
because you've chosen to be scared and crippled by doubt!
If you aren't willing to do what is required for your desires,
how will it ever be acquired?
Do you understand or am I preaching to the choir?
Who cares about what someone else has done in light of what you have to do?
Who cares who came out before you and they got the game sewn up?
How many lifetimes will you give way in lieu of another lifetime of failure?
How many years will you perfect your expertise of doubt?
What's it gonna be? We can already tell which you'll choose
because fruit is the receipt of labour.
Truth is you gon either accept the tasks at hand
or accept the misery of your soul!

Wu Wei

It took me a while to gather my thoughts,
and my being to understand what was meant and intended
by a phrase I saw in a movie that seemed like the simplest yet most
profound usage of words I've heard. "No Mind". Contextually, I saw
this from the context of someone trying to learn a new skill and you could see
that they were overwhelmed- by the learning, the execution and the people
they felt were judging while they thought they were failing. The teacher,
aware as though having gone through this themselves- reassured the pupil
and said "too many mind! then looked sternly at him and said no mind!
The look on the pupils face was even more perplexing than the lesson.
as a thinking thinker, overthinker and all around creative,
how do you get to a state of "no mind". The thought lingered, perplexing
my immaturity as though teasing me about its unattainability.
I didn't pay it any mind, because of the context to which it was brought.
It occurred during the initial stages of learning and I am grateful for always
wanting to learn; there I knew time would reveal in the mystery
and this No Mind concept.

Many years later while writing for The Macabre Erudite series,
I came across a phrase I have no idea how: but the term is Wu Wei
and boom, without chasing, without fighting or worrying; the term
and its meaning felt like we needed to meet. I was aware of several evolutions
that I had gone through, aware of the maturity I had been experiencing
I was constantly overwhelmed, constantly overthinking, overdoubting
and overhesitating and I was over it. I didn't know how to manage
the newness I was going through; I didn't know how to process
the thoughts that were invading my peace. it all felt like everything
was heightened- the sense of failure, the aura of insecurity- the delusions
of fatigue and the reruns of accepting defeat. I related to the character
and the new skill. the constrains of life and its evolutions, the cycle of maturity
and its testings, the darkness of the cocoon and the labour pains of depression.
I've been there, overwhelmed and uncertain; perplexed and baffled, in awe
and confused....unable to make sense of it all and crumbling in the meantime.

There I was, lowkey astral projecting, in the sense of: I know me, my actions
and my defaults- I was guilty of having too many minds. The mind to fight
depression, the mind to know and not being unsure, the mind to bare the pain,
the mind to pass the tests of life's s lessons, the breaking of generational bonds,
the task to treat myself kind- too many minds. All the tasks were necessary
and had to be assessed and addressed, I couldn't just sweep them to the side
for sake of transient peace. I did the best I could, to tackle what whatever it was
when I was cognisant; figuring out how to apply my best, in the scenarios
that came at perilous times. I was rumbling, bumbling and fumbling;
trying to get a grip before the loss of control would even start to show outside
of my overthinking barrier of control. Bogged down, hurt, unsatisfied
and of course being my harshest critic; I often slumped into dejection because
of my inability to control or maintain.

It wasn't until a phone conversation occurred, where I was encouraging a loved one about the process of being whole; how difficult it is because we are trying to do something new with the foundational defaults we've perfected over the course of our life. Our natural "no mind" is chaos and trauma, because that's what we've practiced. We have to identify where we've repeated our mistakes, our wrong doings, identify the mindset we execute them in, look for the scenarios where they happen often and consistently right them so we can create new defaults generating the results we truly desire. Ultimately creating an efficacious effortless mode of being where our experience isn't filled with the same laborious trying when we were in essence practicing.

Until we have searched, found and done the work to undo what we have become-effectively changing our perspective and our responses, only then can the movement towards what we desire be considered non action or as easy as breathing so to speak, better yet mindfully axiomatic. See in the movie, the character was practicing, he was just hampered by the unrealistic burdens albatrossing his entirety. When he was able to conquer the deficiencies in each area, his movement became fluid, mindless and he exerted less energy than he did when we was trying to make it work, trying to get it right, trying to not forget, trying to not quit, trying to belong and trying to impress. From 2004, this idea of "being" stained my psyche and in the end of 2021 I was able to get a better grasp of it. Still learning, myself and mastering the idea therewith.

Explore You, Without Permission

We have grazed deathfully on the insecurities of our invisible prison.
Moment by moment feasting heartily on the emptiness of trauma
that we've acquired a flavourful taste for; so we cower in the crevices
of the corners of irrelevance where we've made out bed of discontentment.
We've locked ourselves out of ourselves while feeding on the scraps of the leftovers
from the feasts we've happily fed lecherous turncoats. From this lonely corner
of misery, we've managed to the impossible in our brokenness,
not to mention the countless times we achieved the unthinkable
for everyone but ourselves. Timelessly, we've accomplished more heroic feats
than any one in Greek folklore for the sake of another,
while failing to give ourselves a fifth of the effort we've given ourselves.

Why, I ask are we willing to go to the ends of the earth for strangers,
family and friends but won't leave the corner of fear for ourselves?
Why have we allotted so much space for tourists to move at will,
on a whim across the expanse of our being. risking violation, heartbreak,
disappointment, and the like- but wimpishly prevent ourselves from exploring
the greatest adventure of our lifetime... ourselves. Why is it, that we only know
what we can do through the recovery from pain? Why is it that we find
the fullness of our powers in anguish, turmoil or hurt? Why, have we so freely
given blank checks of control and pink slips of surrender?
Is it because we have become so used to not being loved enough
that we've raised the standard of our recovery from
the many bouts of lovelessness, so we stubbornly and obscenely
run into another agreement of failure?
I ask, simply because of the parameters we given ourselves
and have reinforces over the years of our existence.
We've had it in reverse the entire time. We've given more to others
than we've ever given to ourselves: more comfort, more allowances,
more space to find themselves, more support for their dreams,
more shoulders to cry on- et cetera, et cetera. While we beg for the same
individuals we gifted whole new worlds to, to give us shelter in the realms
we've given them- only to find ourselves again lonely, dejected
and regretful because we knew better.

So what do we do? We lower the standard of our love in the ways
of how we need and want to be loved to how others can afford to love us.
In doing so we not only settle for less, but over time we force ourselves
to vie for a version of strong affection that never satisfies
the longing we desperately crave. We believe that only what others
have to offer is the best we'll ever get and because we haven't given ourselves
any good measure of the love we wastefully dole out
we setup castles of rue in fortresses of skepticism,
painted in a broken form of arrogance; l, boldly building edifices
whose foundation is anchored in the ignorance
of who we are and the power of us.
We've done all this all while crammed into the nookiest crevice
of obscurity somewhere in the expanse of our being.

We've confined ourselves to the least of everything,
we've ridden ourselves of the beauty that is all of us
while boasting naively about the commodities that we get abused for.
In these parameters we imprison ourself in,
we refrain from being accountable, honest, kind and loving.
Perpetuating the rules of insufficiency to such a high degree
that we never see the meticulous upkeep of the trauma we nurse.
In these parameters, we fail to venture out into the unknown of our being,
too afraid to unveil the potential, maybe. Too afraid to realise
that we never needed what we settled for and we are more than
everything we dreamed we could've been.
These parameters we've set over our entire being handicap how we give,
receive and view love. This is most notably seen when someone loves us
the way we truly need to be loved instead of the affectionate attention
we've bamboozled ourselves into believing is love.
When we are shown this version of love we run and hide,
we doubt the reality of it, the existence of it;
we begin to harshly critique,
more so ourselves and our deservance of it.

Here comes someone whose arrival in our existence gives us
more space to be, more space to take up and be freer than we've been.
Then here we go, looking at the person who opened the invisible cage
we alone see, that we alone have been serenading with songs of misery
and incarceration from, then falsely attribute the freedom to the person
instead of the space of amazing you already came with. Honestly, I get it!
Before this person, this freedom wasn't an option- let alone a possibility.
So we pack our traumas, doubts, hiding our hopes and faiths
dropping trinkets of pain so that if it doesn't work out we can find
our way back to our interminable nook. What proceeds to happen is,
we go sightseeing on this tour of amazing sights and wonders.
Thrilled with this new lease on life and the excitement therewith;
we begin to move more boldly, more comfortably. Maybe this is real,
maybe this can happen- maybe I deserve this and out of left field
comes a separation from this person. This person who you began
this exploration of self with, finding the new things in life
you love experiencing is now gone. All the progress you've made,
all the hope you've had dashed away
because you attributed these new parameters with them.

Truthfully, some of us avoid the activities we did with that person
because of the pain of that departure; we gave them the keys of our being,
they took us on a joyride through the expanse of ourselves and parked
us deeper in our cubbyhole than before. We never knew ourselves,
never understood ourselves and surely never appreciated ourselves.
So how would we have known how far our being extends,
how would we have known the greatness we house within?
We too often fail to learn who we are without the aid of trauma,
too often we fail to explore ourselves without the company of someone
we choose to love. Far too often we've chosen to be escorted in chains,
while being an extra in the journey of our being in this existence.

We never needed another soul to escort us to who are,
we never needed the angst of trauma to explore
`the how amazing our recovery skills are.

You, have always been the stunning and untapped universe,
you have always been beaming with abundance, you've always been more
than the more that you once drew up at the height of your brokenness.
You, are- still the greatest adventure of your lifetime! Explore yourself,
the highs and the lows, travel through the boundaries you first built in fear
and unleash the maximum amount of your YOUness bravely but kindly.
Love yourself enough to know, what moves you and flow in that knowledge.
Love yourself enough to know what brings discomfort; understand the reasons,
find the truth of the root and address it how you need to. Love yourself enough
to know what you want and what you do not. Love yourself to know
what sabotage looks and sounds. Love yourself better than the trauma
you kept up in your heartache and agony. It isn't easy, it won't be,
but you deserve the best version of you in every aspect of your existence
and you are the only person capable of rewarding you of this blessing.
I believe in you, the truest and happiest version of you and I wish you would to.
No matter the path of the journey, please
always remember to never dream below your possibilities
in a world where possibility is in everything.

Rediscover You

My friends, I charge you, to ceaselessly chart the mountains
and caverns of your being! Run freely and bare the entirety
of your soul through the hills and valleys of your entirety.
Hike across the expanses of your various unknowns.
I urge you, with all the joy you have, to travel wanderlustfully the divine
terrain that is you. When you happen upon them, do not be afraid,
instead- feed what you once feared were the monsters
you were once scared of; know now that they are your guides
through the seas and skies that make up all of you!

No matter the weather, let it be known,
the storm in you will never rage into your destruction.
No matter the tempest, it will throw you about,
but it will never toss you into oblivion.
Destiny: YOUR destiny has made you unsinkable,
the guardians of fate also made you undrownable.
Remember, that you are the amazingly bright
and perseverant being whose existence was created to overcome
every obstacle that you may see or face.
Forget not, that every hardship
and hurdle is but an overexaggerated
steppingstone to the better version of you.
Trust, that the healthier and more whole version
of you, is waiting eagerly to be loved aright!
Believe me, the better version of you
is only pending until you decide it isn't.

Unpend... reassess, readdress, redefine
and accomplish all things that you desire!
You are worth the lifetime of your lifetime
to enjoy the lifetime of your life's time.
Know, that you are worth the exploratory beauty
and hidden treasures you will undoubtedly find.
So, I implore you, chart the mountains and caverns of your being;
run freely and bare the entirety of your soul
through the hills and valleys of your entirety;
hike across the expanses of your various unknowns,
for you are the greatest adventure you will ever know.

Entelechenesis

I am the sunrise of my own darkness
the miracle worker conjuring healing elixirs
brewed for the maladies of childhood trauma.
I am the super hero saving myself from my own demise,
the most sought after prize the voice of wisdom
inside counselling the anger and naiveté show.

I now know that I know now,
that I am the pre-eminence of all things legendary;
unswayed and unbothered by the infirmities
of celebrated tragedies... that was me.
No longer the hypochondriac unicorn ailing in a zoo of mules
wailing about the burdens I wasn't supposed to bear,
the albatross hugs that adorned me everywhere
I am stronger by what seemed like mistakes
once disheartened by the relapse and retakes.

I am no longer the christ of the circle
crucifying myself for the betterment of detriment.
No longer the merciful and quiet being
whose being taken for granted or taken for the fool.
No longer do I wait hand and foot
for the hands and feet of them
who delight to showcase the nothingness in me.

I am no longer the insecure, unsure
doubtful and negatively self-speaking
universe crumbling within itself,
I've sent it to the blackhole of oblivion
to be chastised then baptised
then sentenced to be Qhubified
that it may be brought to life anew.

Therefore I am now, the standard
for which all dope is defined.
I am the standard to which all legendary aligns!
I am the pre-eminent diadem of amazing,
the greatest believer of myself
and the greatest achiever I ever met.
I decree and I declare that I in all my dopeness will be
loved regarded appreciated and revered
by all but more so by me.

Qhuxion

the world will not make space for you
you already take up space in its existence;
it has all been equipped with the facilities and wherewithal
to house and withstand the complexities
you've been destined and burdened with.

So reclaim the vastness of your identity
leased and loaned out to lecherous licentious immoral leeches
sucking the life, hope and love out of you
because you time after time doubted
if the world was ready or could handle all the idiosyncrasies
you are so brilliantly plagued with.

Show the world what you've ceaselessly shown yourself.
Know that you did it, take stock in the fact that you did it
and the world will know what you've always known
that you more than just belong....
you are divinely created to manifest
the entirety of your entirety wholly and entirely.

CREATIVITY

IS
A NULL AND VOID CONTRACT

WHEN IT BECOMES COMMON.

From Emily To Me

My beloved, don't just skim through the pages of my life;
share the story of how I tried before I died.
Tell them how I got better I just couldn't share;
how I recited their favourite lines,
that death wouldn't let them hear.
Tell them my struggles were beautiful,
the lessons were hard, but the diamond remarkable!
Tell them, "Write!" Leave no memory untouched;
and when it pertains to "bad writes"; there are no things as such.
Tell them, write in love or in anger at whatever time;
for angry thoughts housed in a closed mind
are the reason for one's death inside.
Tell them to stand tall and remember we glory in the story,
a writer might never go anywhere
but they can take anyone everywhere with just words,
and you, most of all, are the voice that must be heard.
I ask you this: how will they be reached if you won't start the train in fear?
Free yourself and you'll liberate a million faces in a thousand places.
Just remember: many will love your words,
but cherish those who love you in the spaces.

My Love, step forward and be bold, no matter if it frightens you;
even in silence, make sure your actions never mute.
When in darkness, know that the dark
is also a light for all things hidden, brightest of these—YOU!
The light doesn't know the darkness,
it only sees where it isn't; unaware of the length,
breadth and brightness it has behind.
Do not stutter or lazily flash your brilliance—
blind them, then narrate the occurrences during their lack of sight.
Don't be afraid to make your mark, even if it defaces the world;
and if you must, die with your ink dry and pen worn,
not your heart and mind.
Show them there's more hope outside of the world that defines it.
Show them there's more love than their inability to define it.
Be the light, for it never dies; history will fan the flame.
Even when your loved ones have gone you will not be left alone
because we have found the philosophers stone.
Your love,
E.E.D
P.S.—
I couldn't wait for legendary,
but he took to chasing me.
Out of breath, he gave me a stone
sought by Immortality

EARTHQUAKES

Aren't known until they make an impact;
their potential cannot truly be measured,
if they don't ever materialize
or aren't ground shaking ...

of a truth,
I do not know
if these rumblings will have an effect

Nevertheless, may the faults
that brought you this quakening
soulfully resonate and eternally
remain with you 'til time reverses
and history moonwalks into antiquity.

WELCOME TO MY

GRANDSCENDENCE

GRANDSCEND:
TO PERSEVERE VICTORIOUSLY
BEYOND THE DOUBT OF ONESELF

GRANDSCENDING:
THE PROCESS OF CONQUERING
MENTAL MONUMENTS OF FAILURE
CREATED DURING MOMENTS
OF IGNORANCE AND NAIVETÉ

GRANDSCENDENCE:
THE QUALITY OF MASTERY
WHEN ONE HAS OVERCOME THE HINDRANCES
WITHIN THEMSELVES,
ALONG WITH THE CRIPPLING SOCIETAL
AND CULTURAL NORMS
RESULTING IN THE EVOLUTION OF ONESELF

GRAMMERLIN SQUARE

I stand before thee all—
with braggadocio, divine confidence
and unmitigated gall.
I intend to give you, my listeners,
abundantly, wholeheartedly, all of me
with the palpable potency
reminiscent of Niagara Falls.
But above all, with humility now gripping,
nervousness and anxiety trickling,
I hope that fate and creative ingénue
will, in perfect timing, have me on all cylinders...

clicking ...

sounds no longer abound;
this is the pressure that hurts,
creating life out of the deathly silence,
fidgety and hesitant before the verse.
Nerves butterflying like it was the first go-round;
the moment is now, cometh the hour
eager pilgrims awaiting the sound.
A step for epic and confidence sets in
assurance rises and feedback halts its peak
Now, I'm shivering down to the depths of my soul
a dare before a million headlights
anticipating visionary as I speak
waiting for similes to pun metaphors;
breath-taking verbs showcasing
how well noun these life sentences can be.

Here, now you've waited patiently
cometh the man, wielding legendary perpetually
poetic royalty wrapped in eternity.
Be overwhelmed.
His aura permeates the soul
with words that hurt the hurt
'til it brings all that consoles.
Welcome to this Lyrically Alphabetical Soulgery.
Come and see proof of all that you've heard of me
see your reward
The Pensiah and Qhubist
Teyhguwehtehl, the Alqhumizt is here.
Welcome, dear pilgrims, to the forever affair
held at Grammerlin Square.

FOR THE READERS

I do not know where this book finds you or how you came across it,
but I'd like for you to know what it means to me. In a nutshell, this book
is and has been my healing: both the process and the manifestation.
Before I began writing and compiling, I survived a series of unfortunate events
that had me broken and unnerved spiritually, mentally and physically.
I retreated from friends and family. I hid my pain and my glaring
vulnerabilities so I could appear strong. In truth, it was the longest lie I had
helped maintain. I didn't know who to turn to, or if I could even turn.

Every time I thought I was down and out, there was another downer
that put me further under. When anyone attempted to encourage me with the
cliché "up is the only way left to go," I learned "down" can be eternal;
truth be told it was "down" where I spent most of my time, so much so I was
forced to set up camp. It was there, at the rock bottom of rock bottoms,
that I learned the taut feeling of despair and the claustrophobia of hopelessness.
Pain made me clang as it clung closer than lovers clinging their missed loved
ones. I learned to breathe, even when it hurt doing the rounds (inhale/exhale);
and it was there, intermingled amongst the laboured routines, that this
alphabetically cathartic medical meditation ushered itself on a creative
surfboard, riding on a wave of hope; doing gnarly cowabungas
on the forefront of my mind.

The idea was there, some of the material too, but I wasn't ready.
I wasn't whole, nor was I close. In a sense, it was still loading.
I found myself once, years ago. I knew me, but before this book,
I seemed rather unfamiliar. I was me, but not me enough
to meet the task before me. I had to re-find me, wherever I was,
to see whoever I'd become during the time I ignored me.
This book helped; it helped me re-find and then refine me, and in the
refining, I was able to redefine me. You have your own journey ahead of you.
I only hope you diligently seek with the intention to find, then meticulously
refine, only to honestly redefine, if not define, yourself. Life is your journey;
find, address and repair you. Your happiness depends on it.

GAS MONEY

I can't tell how long it's been, but they say "the journey of a thousand miles begins with a single step." I kinda believe that the journey hasn't begun until you have something to look back at and still decide to continue. I haven't measured the time, nor have I counted the times I've looked back, since I embarked on this dark road. It appears each step taken brought me away from the sun, as I didn't see light or hope when I stared into the utter abysmality of the unknown, and its seemingly incontrovertible uncertainty. I was a writer of sorts with an amateur style (still, maybe); nevertheless, I was hungry to see a generation that I'd probably never meet recite and quote my words, my lines and my verses with the same verve I envisioned as I wrote them.

See, I wanted that Shakespearean sort of legacy. Not the kind where we dispute whether Shakespeare was the actual writer, no, I wanted all the notoriety, the reverence of being regarded highly. I didn't care if he was overrated or underrated, I wanted the overwhelming inundation of my material flooding school books, classes, libraries and history for generations to come. I wanted it into unquenchable desperation; felt as though if your work was on any sort of medium, that was a great feat, and for that, I was jealous of every writer or poet or performer who got cheers for their craft. I envied them, not because of their talent, but for the responses they received (still, maybe).

I wanted it—all of it, every snap and handclap. I wanted the momentum they had to gather to cheer; hell, I even wanted whatever electrical signal that triggered in their brains to respond to what anyone else wrote. This fuelled me on my journey. I didn't know where I was going; I just knew I had gas money. Every open mic, every picture of a performer, a post or a reshare of a video by anyone of any talent, every like AND EVERY TAG—sigh.

Maybe you'll stay the entire trip; maybe you'll find solace or relatability on a particular avenue, lane, road or stroll; maybe you'll confront yourself in the alley. Maybe you don't find anything you like or appreciate. Maybe this is your gas money. Safe travels, my dear pilgrims. Safe travels.

The Motto

-I aim for that which
-no mere mortal can physically
-obtain or reach; knowing that
-where hands and failures do not succeed, -
-I will granscend beyond all limits
-with words and speech...

-so as creativity beckons
-and legendary's call is near
-I will answer to the higher plea
-and as art bequeaths
-I humbly pray
-my surreal impact -
-eternally stains the air

Akiim

Ea Incipit

WELCOME TO
GRAMMERLIN SQUARE

HOME OF
THE GRANDMENTALSTATION

ALL ABOARD
THE GRANDSCENDENCE

FIRST STOP:

The Mind of a Man

Both beautiful and detestable.
It is filled with a barbaric horde of thoughts
that are immensely cruel and reek of savagery.
It relents not, neither does it care,
nor does it want for the safety of my sanity.
It does as it pleases, justifies its faults
and scrutinizes its strengths.
What's strength is weakness and what's weakness
is both strength and flaw.

The mind of a man takes him on
non-hallucinogenic trips where sobriety
is inversely described, and while it damages,
it's also what the innate nature of my being
prescribes. Its autonomy is dependent of my willingness
to justify its sovereignty over my rebellious quintessence.
I'm both captor and captive, Pinocchio and Geppetto,
simultaneously both judge and defendant.
Contrarieties and contradictions are intertwined
then plaited to suit the situational irony
of the ever-increasing awareness of my mortality
and the insignificance of my reality... it wears me down,
and it wears me out–the mental struggle, that is–
an uphill battle on a mountain slope steeped with impossible,
dressed in spectacular mirages of peace and success.

This mind of mine is intrinsically Pandora's playground,
simultaneously prison and amusement park–
the reason for peace and the cause of its disturbance.
It is my joy and my displeasure,
the boldness of my anarchy and the testament of my humility.
The strong root of my love and the grim reaper of my affections.
The mind of a man, both Troy and a self-awarding Trojan horse,
individually all participants of Stockholm's syndrome.
Woe is me, as we are undone and alone–abroad and at home.
This mind is a mine unearthed.

A QUILT OF BROKENNESS

I'd like to share a story, in truth, a series of stories
filled with sequential melancholy
and replete with calamity.
These are chock
with judgement and destitution,
a story where pain was a best friend,
Misery was a mother and Hurt nurtured
more than Love ever would.
Are you here still?

Would you read a story of how one could sacrifice
for the goodness of others
but couldn't afford forgiveness of self?
An adventure where silence
told more stories than a lie ever did?
Where to forget is the most requested gift,
simultaneously the most denied?

Would you come to a place
where hope survives on dreams
and dreams don't exist?
A place where you fit in only to be used
as cleaning, cooking and sex tools;
a place where you can't forget
but can be forgotten?
Would you read such story? Tell the truth!

The individuals who, along with myself,
have come together to share
all that we've gone through in hopes
that you, dear reader, won't make our mistakes
but will be emboldened to be free
from the shackles of love and duty
in the face of abuse and blatant disregard.

We present a quilt of brokenness
to cover a multitude of shards
because when they cover you,
your wounds match each stitch
and it brings comfort after all.
Comfort for your soul from a cover that consoles
even better than your despair.
Please. Come and see.
Come and read, come be free.

WHAT IS FEAR? (I)

"what ails your soul?
What procrastinatory disease
seeps through your quintessence
and cripples it so?
What promises bestowed upon you
have you rescinded?
What versions of happiness have you repelled?
How many times have you Rapunzeled
your potential into abject oblivion?
Will you tell?
Will you share how many mistakes
you've fallen in love with,
how many regrets have been birthed
in sheer discomfort?
How many times have you sacrificed your sacrifices
only to burn on the altar of
"I should've" and "I knew better"?
What is fear but the culmination of pump fakes
and exquisite mental assent
crippling the prevalent thought
of doubt in your mind?
What has it cost you? Are tears the receipts?
Do you know?
What is fear?

The Barter System

an exchange for an exchange
though an uneven one;
complicity for silence
violation for pleasure
decadence for innocence.
prey sacrificed
and this private deflowering
sets the stage for public demise.

naïveté being fleeced
as the culprit pounces
when unsuspecting sleeps.
a dog for his bone,
his pet, his treat.
cruelty unveiled, purity ravaged
as novice thespians
act crimeless on stage.

guiltless in guile
deviance with a smile,
monster vile and deranged
youth estranged. hidden in darkness.
unpunished deeds
fruits of barbarism
breeds regretful seeds blossoming
from the misdeeds of missed deeds.
shh it's just a secret. just a touch.
its repeated, such and such
a little sneak with no peeps
(pun intended)

an exchange for an exchange
chastity maligned
Adam and eve unaware of the signs
the desire to be loved
miscreants took advantage of...
love for silence
a touch of compromising
violations quieted
a corrupt system
where only the victim pays.
welcome to a patriarchal society.
oh lord what a shame.

The Pain in My Smile

I wade, writhing uneasily, squirming even;
there's something missing, it's conflicting
as I reach for nothing,
but I know there's something looming in the distance.
Is anyone there, is anyone listening ...
to the gloom and the sorrow in my smirk,
the heartache in my humanity ...
the conformity to be alright,
the desperation to be strong in front of you?
Behind bathroom stalls, I cry ...
I try to hide, but in me, the truth creaks
Do you hear the discomfort,
as teeth show their hypocrisies?
Blatant fallacies fooling the oblivious friends
who never really cared for me,
who were never there for me
to ever understand the pain in my smile...

How can they profess they love me?
When they don't see the love in me decomposing,
I am only posing as I hide behind
a short burst of chuckles,
while nail biting and knees buckle
because myself and I aren't a happy couple ...
do you feel the cringe in the wrinkles,
and the suffering in the arches,
the arches contorting and distorting what my heart is.
I can no longer love like I used to;
and trust me, I've tried;
to go beyond the internal persecution of doing
the maintenance work of these gargantuan lies.
You haven't seen, or realized,
with those desensitized eyes,
this anguish of mine,
and as I continue to tell you I'm fine,
in hopes you calculate the error of these lines;
I'll sit here bearing
the pain in my smile

Blatant Subliminals

Hidden within a dialect is my accumulated pain.
To the grief experienced, my soul is regrettably chained.
My speech propels a vision not everyone can see
woven intricately inside my verbiage
is an unheard plea of "Please Help Me!"
I speak a spoken language others learned not to talk
woven intricately inside
are words uttered where only torture stalks.

"I need to be alone" is what they hear from my mouth,
upon disappearing my mind unleashes
a shriek that my mouth lets outs.
My heart's ready for the love but the Warden named Pain
is too cold and insensitive to let her out.

Hidden within a dialect is my constant cry for help.
My plight goes unnoticed
each and every time the previous word was next.
Word after word, my pain
is pronounced with deft annunciation
Pronounced skillfully as though
my attempts to propitiate my audience
will ultimately release me from this grief
and reward me emancipation.

As I let loose a barrage of words formed by legions of letters
my turmoil takes flight
as though in mid-speech it miraculously grew feathers.
A heightened subconscious is lowered by what's present.
Uttered with the unction that I be revealed, because for far too long
my audience's comprehension seems incapable of function.

Hidden within a dialect is my humble and lowly plea.
For all who have an ear to hear the clamour of feebleness that is all of me.
Hidden within a dialect is the simplicity of a complex plea,
woven intricately inside is a map of how to get to the

b   b
     r   r
         o   o
             k   k
                  e
             n   n

                  m   e

HIDDEN DISGUST (HID IN DISGUST)

There it remains, to the side
as though in an existential time out of sorts.
I yell, "why don't you come out the corner?"
Obstinately recalcitrant yet obedient to the cause and my necessity,
they refuse and just stay there, not turning or crying about injustice,
not protesting the corporal punishment and the trauma it presents.
I despise it, and they're aware, they should've known better,
come out of the corner- but they remain stubborn
"I know you hear me, you just don't care!
Do you know the pain you caused us?
You won't even look at me.
Why were you so naive so foolish and so innocent
'til naiveté was the cost of your innocence?"
They just stay there, not moving. Not paying attention to my anguish,
not giving ear to the derogatory words that get hurled.
Again I yell, "You are disgusting, and you appal all of me,
for what you did, everybody needs their own corner
and that's where you'll stay forever, you hear me, lil' kid?"
(but how could they have known? it doesn't matter. they should have.)
And I don't even care that you were a kid. I hope you get comfortable.

Just look at you, you disgrace me you're an embarrassment.
Why don't you say anything? Answer me, you... you little whore!
You're a slut, and it's true; you even stand like a slut!
How can you live with yourself?
Don't you feel guilty about what you did?
How could you? After all those years of learning about stranger danger
and your parents telling you to tell them if anyone touched you;
They were home, and you were scared.
Why didn't you yell then? You wanted it; you liked it, didn't you?
Admit it. You saw the pretty girls at school and wanted the attention they got.
Look what Christmas gifts they brought, you unwrapped and unrapt
pleasure unfair and unsure; they enjoyed
while you confused and scarred and scared.

She just stands there, in the corner and never moves or makes a sound
and only when I'm most broken does she turn around.
She senses my despair and sighs,
begins to cry as she sees the waterfalls coming from my eyes.
She takes her first step and I lose control
a piece of me requited as she establishes her sole.
You should've said something, now it's too late,
I'm broken, as the invasions made me a POW in my own estate,
captive to these painful memories, that so often bring me low.
She always knows when to just walk over,
never saying a thing, as I hurl expletives and derogatory words towards her.
She steps still, and walks towards anger
and resentment, despite what she often hears.
She's always there when I need her to console me and hold me.

WHAT IS FEAR? (II)

What is your definition of Fear?
Pray tell, how does it define you?
Do you know? What is it that truly scares you?
What drives you, into paralyzing hesitation?
How do you react to your weaknesses,
when they approach you? Do you cower often?
Where do you seek refuge?
What are the causes of your dismay?
Does death fear you, or are you afraid to die?
Are you afraid of dying
without ever making any semblance of an impact?
Is it possible that you're intrinsically nervous
that death will be your greatest significance?
Does being or remaining a failure excite you?
Does it tame you? Do you know?
What prevents you from doing your best
or achieving what you need?
What impedes your dreams with such freezing dread?
Why dream goals and wake up to do nothing about them?
What manner of existence are you a hostage in
when all you do is wake up
only to snort unrealized dreams again?
What is the cost of your fear?

CLAUSTROPHOBIA

I'm stuck in here and I can't get out
unable to find a way that'll let me live,
so I keep myself in a corner within.
Unable to scream loud enough,
in hopes that the pain lessens.
It never does—an inaudible lesson.
Pondering escape in an upright foetal position,
stressing, I feel dirty and ashamed;
I cringe when I hear that voice call my name.
I need to get out; can anyone hear me?
I'm screaming in silence, banking on hope,
still so bankrupt, a walking cry for help.
My soul signals SOS in Morse code
a language we don't know and it shows.
Taking a million steps forward in the same position
is merely an escalator that never comes back up.
I wish my self would come back
back to hope, back to life
back when things were aright;
but I'm just stuck here
unable to get out or see an exit.
I wish there was an open-door button
(my luck would likely be that it'll cease to work once I press it).
Have you ever felt so alone, and lonely
that even the most comfortable places seem so unhomely?
imagine the one place where you're be free to be,
free to just breathe, free to partake in the bitter slices of peace,
'cept, here you feel your worst fears repeating,
coming back full circle as though it's reheating.
The pain, closing in, on you and everything
feeling the discomfort of the déjà vu all over again.
Reliving the violation from the unpaid tolls of Life's highway;
It's closing in, with no refrain, here comes the fear of being alone,
then the fear of darkness and the fear of rain,
multiplied by the nightmares of being hurt again.
Sittin' up, knees to chest with my arms around me
making every wish to get out
yet still I remain, closed in, while life is closing.
I'm still hoping and barely coping
with all the turmoil that gathers within;
bullied outside constantly
only to feel like a foreigner in my own skin
all while my deepest darkest is closing in.
and I'm still tormented by the cruelty of him,
not just the pandemonium within.

WHY I BANG MY PILLOWS

I reach out for help, yet they all mock and jeer.
Know they not for the past couple of years
no one has been there?

(Been Where)?

here... to stay and allow me the peace of enjoying life.
They all came to steal my joy away,
and in pain, they let me writhe.
So I bang my head against the pillows
because it softens my every blow;
insensitive to my awkward emotions, their love for me just froze.
Easily the humans leave and make absent their presence,
while I who truly cared, am left to pick up the shattered pieces
of my loves abstract essence.

head hits pillows

I need someone, but it seems as though she isn't
ready for a friend; she, who is me,
seems to be a plague, for time after time
they who are about be infected
by the infestation of my love again.
I'm befuddled, mulling "will the loneliness ever end?
Will companionship be made whole
by someone whose love can mend?"
So I bang my pillows for no one will ever console me;
therefore, repetitiously, I bang my head
'til the force of movement dwindles slowly,
and as the momentum rapidly decreases,
I sleep somewhat peacefully upon pillows
of tears, that typify shattered pieces.

head hits pillows in tears

I bang my pillows for my uniqueness
no one will understand.
The barrage of completely weird idiosyncrasies
I happen to be, no ordinary human is able to withstand.
I ... I bang my pillows while tears hug my face.
I pray for the day my feathery friends declare abstinence,
and loneliness will find its place.
I cry for the pain experienced,
I cry for the love I've never known,
for all who profess love to me
have found themselves another home.
They've found themselves someone to love them
and have left me here, to fend for love on my own.

I love you pillows

I need not your pity, for these scenarios
are advanced, amplified versions of déjà vu.
They who profess to be with me,
no matter how much truth is in them;
I will waste no faith by believing you.

Therefore I bang my pillows, for they serve
a purpose in my comfort.
So when it pertains to relationships,
my damp feathers always come first;
for times of loneliness are truly
when I understand my pillow's worth.

So I bang my head against my pillows,
for no one will ever console me;
therefore, repetitiously, I bang my head
'til the force of movement dwindles slowly;
and as the momentum rapidly decreases,
I sleep somewhat peacefully upon a pillow of tears
that typifies shattered pieces.
I'll bang my head against my pillows
'til the presence of positive
and loyal company increases.

The Therapist

I'm supposed to sit here
telling you, with your PhDs,
about what happened to me,
and you, with your vast
experience of listening
should tell me what's wrong.
It's the same ole song.
Everybody's an expert on everyone else,
especially with the peoples they haven't met.

Tell me, if I don't tell you

where did I go in my mind
when I left my body behind?
Tell me how I relived every invasion
to just lay there lifeless
with the spoils of war in me emblazoned.

I fought for life, while he tried
to place an unwanted kind in mine,
as if my existence wasn't already filled with strife.
He shoved more than my pride aside,
my defences infiltrated,
my walls battered
and my being shattered.

the rapist forced my therapy,
while my therapist forced
my recollection of the tragedy;
a rock and a hard place.
Playing tough, yet still
too broken to bluff–
the blinking game
with a proud poker face.

Tell me what did he look like?
What stench was on his breath?
How many times did I run out of soap and loofahs
when the requirement for clean could not be met?
How many times do I wake up to cold sweats
and replays being re-raped? Misfortune plays DJ
as I hear "don't scream. Don't move or I shoot you."
So I didn't, and he still shoots.
Tell me if I don't tell you
what my favourite colour was, favourite song,
favourite time of the day,
and then having it all turned wrong?

Tell me, what class made you able
to relate and appreciate?
Tell me, which of your tragedies
makes you the sorcerer and
maker of elixirs for all my remedies?

Tell me, you therapist.
You ask me to remember;
they told me never to forget.
Are you the rapist?
Do you have paragraphs of solutions
in your therapist playlist?
Imagine going to family get-togethers
and all you are able to say is, "don't play this."

And you expect me to just sit here
as you try to relate like you were there?
Is this how sadists get their rocks off;
getting dressed to listen to violence
of the violated whose mind,
shocked by horror,
works in ways too tireless to recover?

I'm just supposed to sit here
and listen to you tell me why,
reliving a moment in time
when, every second passed,
I had wished I'd just die...
so tell me, who are you,
the therapist or an accomplice?

Robin N. Timassy

It was a business card that caught my eye.
His repertoire was padded, no one to contest the negatives—too perfect.
Something had to give. A convicted cynic, I became client.
Somehow mesmerized by the pullover wool that made me sheep-like.
He had the words, and it satiated every doubt I ever had.
God, he was dreamy. Looking like all I'd need and all I ever missed.
I had to plunge; this leap of fate was worth the risk.
Just like that, I signed off on heartbreak with just a flick of my wrist.

Love was a Ponzi scheme for patsies who chose
to invest their emotions haphazardly.
I was merely a connoisseur of misery; my skill was sublime.
My clients were compliant, then reliant; they made a bevy of mistakes:
mismanagement put them in debt every time, forcing withdrawals
and pointless deposits. They were handicapped, disguised as hopeless romantic...
easy candy. The setup was classic, providing promises pending payment,
and the more they gave, the greater the promises. The facade meticulous
and the sorcery exhaustive. It was just too easy.

He created believers out of the heartbroken.
He gave faith to the most abject despondents
who rummaged through agony, daring to attempt to love again.
He knew all the right words; he swooned and confused,
rebuffed and flummoxed, all the skills needed to disarm safety and caution.
I was enamoured and magicmatised.
I created outlets that would lead to manifested dreams.
It was all too real... pain was the alarm of my soul that I could never snooze.
I was played, placing my heart in the hands of Love,
whose strung tunes turned me into a dancing fool.

It was a fool's market, and they came rushing in,
blinded by the glitter of a golden chance.
He leveraged his clients into soulkruptcy,
unbothered by his dastardly ways.
I despise that crooked smile realising that we were all
the favourite candy to a spoiled child.
He came in as a master key, code breaker,
and he soothed every warning that was used
to detect the symptoms of unwanted pains.
He did so easily, all for selfish gain.
Masking the failures of all my past former loves
with success, 'twas as though all their
attempts combined to form this super failure.
He took me to never-seen heights of love and euphoria,
something I longed for, it wasn't long before love capsized
and sank deeper than disappointment ever could.
I'm ashamed at the savagery of his game.
I still, to this day, say the alphabet without using the letters in his name.

He took everything because it was all I had to give;
he gave me the reason then took the very logic embedded within.
I trusted him with more than I could ever imagine: hope,
love and happily every afters, late night stares and belly aching laughter.
I tore down walls, broke down highly classified secrets,
and he devastated my need for intimacy, brought ruin to my emotion.
I fell–hook, line and sinker. I fell for the hope of thrills,
unaware of the danger numbing my gills. He took my breath away...
then took his efforts away.
I'm still hopeful he may return someday;
oft times being lonely is worse than being played.

I hear his name, and it scares and scars
my heart, seared and tarred
possibilities betrayed manifestations,
and all its capabilities marred by this deceit.
Married to receipts of pain,
I have become irascible in every facet of the word.
If you see the signs, it's probably him.
Good looking, exactly what your eyes like,
so it's disarming and you'd give him innumerable chances.
A way with words because that's what he'll do.
He's everything you've ever wanted, maybe even more:
perfect and dreamy as though he came from dreams you've seen.
If you've see anything like this, run, dear child, run.
He's made up of all the curves
and swerves your guardian angel saved you from,
except this time she too swoons
for this man who will rob you of all your love.
Saving for Mr. Right and no one will save you, save you!
You're only a ploy and a play, a distraction,
by the way and that's where he'll leave you, by the way.
So run from the butterflies and urge to flirt,
run from making down payments
with the fountain of bliss beneath your skirt.
Run from this company; it's their policy to ruin and run amok.
You'll think it's fortune you ran into, when it's out of luck.
Heed my warnings and avoid this masculine misery,
especially if his name is

Robin N. Timassy.

Sit & Play: Robin's Tale

She bows before me in surrendered bliss,
anticipating smudge tattoos
from all the fingerprints, from every fingertip
as they, with each touch, sing divine lullabies
that seduce and make intimate love
with the virgin synapses of her obeisant mind.
In all her royalty, she is submissively mine.
A classic painting, tainted by painters
who used loved to revile and defile
this illustrious masterpiece
that effortlessly transcends sublime.
But see her, here now, destroyed
and so she kneels again before me,
with lowly eyes hesitant, but offering
herself to be completely mine.
And though it hurts to tell her no,
I haven't the words, for it brings much
discomfort attempting to hinder her guilty pleasure.

So I stopped, hoping to breathe and be free
from the guilty feel, yet still I couldn't help
but give in to the need for this instrument to bleed,
so I seethe, this harmony of wicked affection
and forbidden love, and again I began to play,
but in the most passionate way.
Though all the notes brought me
despair and grand illusions, still I played
these tunes of heartbreak and confusion
with a heavy heart and a mind
filled with Disney clichés and childish delusions.
And she just sits there, eager for me to use
her tattered heart, scarred body, and dishevelled mind,
this soul's a poor patchwork of human design.
With nothing left, what else could she lose
as she's been pieced together
over time in layaways and IOUs?

For years, she's paid the price of betrayal and lies,
apprehensive to trust anyone who professes love,
she bombards them with a barrage of whys.
Why me? Why now? Why love? Why us? Why forever?
Why marriage and why trust? Completely?
Conflicted between truth and lust,
she gives in and gives the scraps scraped from within,
only to be played on another day, to her dismay,
by some guy who came in disguise at the right time
as Mr. Right, and again she's left alone
after missing all the right wrong signs...

I'm frustrated...
For I do not glory in playing love,
but I'm in way too deep and I'm falling still.
How could she not know this love is for real?
I'm not trying to play, love; this love I have
isn't an act, I don't "play love"...

I love you, but I'm stuck as you just sit there
so nonchalant about being used.
As I play this sombre tune that, to you, sounds good
because you "feel" something
you're accustomed to, so much so it's inaudible.
You feel and I feel, yet we feel differently;
you enjoy being played,
and I am the virtuoso of my own misery.
Only ... because I love you,
there'll never be an end to this tune.
Keeping you happy is what I aim to do.
But she just sits there
as I strum every millimetre of her pain.
Though failing to convince love of us,
determined, I sit here for another day
playing love, in hopes that the power of
my love breaks through and that my love
loves back one day. Until then
she kneels, while I sit & play.

What is Fear? (III)

Why cry about what you want,
but won't do what it demands?
Why have demands,
if you aren't willing to meet them?
What drives you? What drove you?
Why are you still only in the parking lot
in your mind, let alone life?
Why haven't you left yet?
How much longer will you
causally go along for the ride?
Why are you alone in the passenger seat?

Is this fear?

Fear of the future or fear of the unknown?
What moment are you waiting for?
What feeling have you not felt?
What version of emptiness do you crave?
Why are you still here? Why is there no change?
Have all your ambitions ceased in the face of hardships?
Were they really hardships or just you being lazy?
Are you fearful and lazy?
Or are you hardworking and fearful?
What version of fear captivates you?
What is your fear?

Heaven in a Bottle

Elysium was paid for with the hard work of its adoring follower,
a commoner whose animated foot movement
travels with no great commission
to dignify such confusing and ritualistically beleaguered worship.
Never a set meeting, just sweat pellets and dehydration,
dedicated missionary work in taverns,
brothels and other god-filled places.
The stumbling preacher, preaching sermon after sermon
while clarity is never seen,
fumbling words with a conduct obscene
and outright disorderly.

The elusive god of a mortal,
continually hidden from public view;
however, intimacy is manifested
as this deity is always financially accessible.
Halos are quickly thrown to the floor
once eureka has been uncapped and uncovered;
it's smothered, ready to be released at his beckoning.
For that which is in it, he becomes fanatical,
more so overcome with its unstable spirit.
Pouring out graciously over the issues of life
that it would temporarily fix, it gives to its most loyal beings
, a blurred state of mind and deluded speech.
Spilling spirits as he is unable to maintain,
whether it be in discourse or on feet,
a staggering waltz he manoeuvres in his inebriated masquerade,
going on and on, much ado about nothing in his witless tirade.
Rambling enthusiastically while he plays a Chinese master,
each step solidifies the testimony and revelation of disaster...
drunken apocalypse.

See him as he tarries, while in his hands he carries
that which binds him as if married,
then impels him to harry every Tom, Dick, and Garry.
A reality estranged, sobriety he evades.
Pity not the fool as he testifies
about a good life struggling with his stool:
a crude vestige of virility, clinging lifelessly
to some pseudo-reality,
mental brutality and emotional barbarism.
He shakes and stutters involuntarily,
as if struck with shocking aneurisms.
No euphemism can be used
to adequately describe his relentless pessimism
misconstrued for optimism;
aid is needed for his misguided mannerisms, poor thing.

Pitiful, this sight, as convinced is he who tries with all his might
to persuade the ignorant masses about that which he'd been sleight.
Heaven in a bottle is not all its twisted or pulled off to be,
for to limbo that which is inevitable is permissible for misery
to creep in and overrun peace forcefully.
See, here it creates a rambling coward,
who constantly tries to swallow his way to comfort haphazardly.
Perpetual lip service, right on time as he tilts his head back
without looking to the sky, hoping that through syncretism,
Mnemosyne will be lax and aid in his forgetfulness tonight.
Hoping and praying sorrow is drowned out,
reality diluted, good sense polluted and a life uprooted,
defenseless against the truth of a thing,
with heaven in his hands, he breaks out and sings
no particular hymn,
just the suppression of disappointment
festering within.

Dissatisfied, stupefied and petrified,
afraid to confront inadequacies,
misplaced priorities and negligence,
scared to see or feel that which needs be,
he rebels against intelligence–
a marathon runner, running into the proverbial wall,
staggering fiercely to anyone one bored enough to entertain his call.

The bumbling idiot who makes sense in his own head
trots a path on which no sober man treads.
Inexpensive is this heaven, no memory of doctrines,
for this repetition conforms discretion,
leaving unfortunate yet still funny and lasting impressions.
Consider how he staggers still,
not entirely filled with the desecrating spirit
indwelling in him, acting through him, moving him.

All hope abandoned, misfortune embraced
reality skirted, Shangri-La replaced,
utter hopelessness clutches the heart
and it disassembles his intellect;
unable to reflect and correct,
truth he deflects and rejects common sense.
All for a frail and feeble sense of security,
assuredly heaven shan't ever be seen
by such an incredibly pathetic and brittle being.
Entertain the idiot only to laugh, for to guffaw is sure.
The holy bottle yet again is empty; therefore,
heaven has been evicted once more,
the search complete set to repeat,
for evasion has its lustre and allure.

Punch Drunk

It's been a clinic here tonight, folks,
hard to watch the blatant savagery
of this throat-gripping routine.
Not much of a contest though,
and there goes another right and a left,
followed by a flurry of fists that have yet to miss.
This rematch is worse than the previous battles
we've witnessed between the two,
just a thorough bull-dozing and complete mayhem tonight,
look ladies and gentlemen, as he revisits old wounds like a check-up.
A one sided flogging this bad hasn't been seen since
the good Lord Jesus took one for the team.

The mercilessness is unending,
as he seems to be literally mopping the floor
with what's left of his opponent.
You just have to sit back in disbelief
when you look at the sheer size and strength of this man.

Boy, let me tell you, he's going all out tonight!
What a sight to see, ladies and gentlemen! You can follow us
worldwide tonight with hashtag #heavyrightsleepywife
#fightforyourlife and #aintnoequalrightsbih;
just look at the love he takes in delivering every blow,
ironic how the love he uses to pummel
is the love he's walloping out of his opponent.
I see what you did, but did you see just that?

That last shot might just be the proverbial nail in the coffin, folks!
He took everything he had left, placed it squarely on the jaw—
a punch packed like Santa's sleigh before Boxing Day.
But wait a minute, folks! This fight isn't yet over,
as they're getting up they're coming back into the fight.
I don't know if you can call that a fight;
it's almost merciless if it wasn't so entertaining.
One user posted "Rocky couldn't have survived this,
even if he wrote the script."
There's some truth in it; the only problem: this whooping
is real and Rocky isn't.
Speaking of real, that's what it's been, people.
The police and the ambulance are now on site.

We wanted to help, but we don't
get in between the ordeals of husband and wife.

Brenda Had Another Baby

A good woman was decked down
by her black red bottom stiletto pumps
that matched her red cheeks and black eyes;
hope and strength now absent, for here lies
a once phenomenal woman who no longer finds
the strength inside to rise ...
Here she's laid bare, before her husband and her demise:
a barbaric and trifling kind of man who happens to be my father.
Why am I not surprised (deep sigh) ... to see
a man too afraid to embrace the responsibilities of maturity,
so he persuades her pregnant stomach
to donate a seed offering using sarcastic hands;
he aids her nightmare with heavy strikes of authority.
Blow after blow led to blow after blow,
heavily sober on insecurities and coke,
had mom taking different versions of hits to the nose.

Crooked white lines led to straight right hands from an addict,
always seeking a fix without ever mending the issue
his problem usually snorts or sticks.
He loves her passionately with intoxicated punches,
Muay Thai kicks and forced secretions of HIV and syphilis.
She won't leave, hoping he'll revert to the man she married,
the glory of who he used to be (something she knows she will never see).
But paralyzed beneath him she lies, a battered wife
struggling to protect my life with all her might, whimpers "don't! Please!"
But yank after yank, repeatedly as the hanger tears organs,
she viciously bleeds, then no longer breathes.
Finally, I'm in daddy's hands then down the chute he throws me.

As I slide down, no playground, avoiding hefty glad-bag missiles
then landing around semen stuffed condoms,
holy books and thanksgiving turkey half-cooked.
It's unfair as I lie here;
I'm greeted by cracked crack pipe pieces, heroin needles and feces;
I'm gagging as discomfort increases ... and hope ceases,
all while an onslaught of glad bags are repeated ...
and I, like my mother, lay in the fetal position ... defeated.
I ... was painfully evicted without ever getting a chance to be an individual.
This can't be real: reduced to trash and made to feel worthless
by a man already proven to be:
this bastard of a man who symbolizes the world you live in,
ever ready to eliminate whatever causes
you discomfort & disrupts your peace...
Clearly this will never cease, but if it did,
when will the human race be less selfish and mean?

Plagued by self-inflicted insecurities and the need to be pleased,
the harsh reality of poverty and the desperation of greed;
simultaneously, you abort your own growth's process
only to support & revel in the success of people you'll never know,
while being envious and evil to the ones close to you.
I can't say I regret not being able to grow around such a colossal disgrace;
what am I to learn, when we are too proud to be helpful,
but out of a thirst for power... we steal, kill and rape,
out of vengeance for petty reasons we retaliate with unbridled hate,
and give STDs the only time we give each other AID(s)?

How am I to feel when I'm dying with cures meant to be shared with the public?
Would I have been aborted if my parents knew that the remedies
they suffered from were the miracles I was born to come with?
I'm just another saviour, betrayed and aborted before his chance to save the world,
and honestly, I'm glad I wasn't born in this hell hole called "Earth";
and on behalf of myself and the billions ...
that never saw life after birth, because we weren't allowed to be born,
because you ungrateful ... immature ... and inconsiderate assholes
could never appreciate the importance of our worth.

SURVIVE

When you love something, you let it go.
when it comes back to you, it's yours; if it doesn't, that's the end.
Well, these swings always said "return to sender,"
as they let go, it comes again. I've accepted these flings as mine,
as all bring back to mind the remedy for bruised ribs and black eyes:
heavy mascara, sunshades and Mona Lisa smiles.

I remember when we went swinging
but forgot the breadcrumbs to go back
before they were the sole ones slinging swings and flinging things
to hinder the anger within that was aroused
by someone else. And while the guilty and unarmed slept,
I went to bed with laboured breaths.
"Don't make it obvious; he'll do it again. Shut up, stupid girl.
Don't wake him up; you know how he gets".

How could I leave? Just look at how peaceful he is when he sleeps,
how happy he is when he eats.
This love of mine, for whom I gave up my career-calling,
my gift and my life, always comes through
to remind me how good I actually am;
as I cringe every time they raise a hand and I scream believably
'til they hug and squeeze me needfully and I forgive so easily.

I was an artist, and my inspiration was everyday life.
Ironic how the right to be right was followed by rights
which seemed now to be an established rite
that no one you love could write.
But here, I play the theatrical part
of an aging actor playing dead for the sake of life,
who now has the privilege of her life imitating her art.
Fake to die, only to live somewhat of a demeaning life ...
Exit stage, pretend and survive.

THE WAILING

Have you ever heard the story of Atlas
as she struggles all alone, crying as she labours
to shoulder the weight of this depressing globe?
She hides her tears, hoping her weeping
makes no sound, though her searched with all her might;
there still wasn't a location where strength could be found.
Envision a broken woman so weak
when her tears fall they break apart the ground.
Pride kills her inside, so she poses
in the most crippling stance,
all in attempts to keep up a deceptive appearance.
But if they could tell the truth,
what would they say if these tears could speak?
What adjective would describe them,
if waterfalls could feel?
How would you console a woman
if you couldn't mute these tears that scream?
Would you ignore her if you saw
the misery these tears release?

Would you help if you knew it was me?

Because if these tears could feel,
they'd experience a nation too impoverished
to want food for themselves,
so they pass on crumbs, just to pass on crumbs,
to the youngest one with a line so long,
by the time it arrives, the youngest child has died.
Do you know the extent of this grief when
not enough food or water has passed between teeth
and hunger takes deadly selfies daily, posing as full stomachs
while starvation is measured by tapeworms and mass graves?
Death comes and death stays, and mother nature
continues her insensitive ways when
vultures carry on for carrion
and St. Jude rejects accept death 'til
they carry on as carrion ...

Don't you see me struggling?
Won't you help, please?

Because if these tears had the chance,
they'd be betrayal versed as Shakespearian soliloquies,
laced with prolific complexities of Aristotelian speech.
Do you feel these tears as they masquerade
as the façade of peace, feigning to be meek
but reeking with deceit as they butcher without grief,
celebrating mass murder behind the burps of a national feast?

What I mean is ... if they could be,
they'd double as double agents,
teary Benedict Arnolds heavily cascading
a crumbling defense; hypocrisy peaks then leaks
before bursting through a smiling pretence.
Truth is, these tears ain't loyal, and the proof is
if they could, they'd be jealousy and envy
between friends who went their separate ways:
a friendship turned cold by turncoats
because the fabric of love was cut by
the same Brutus blade that had Caesar slain ...

Can't you see these tears are the end of me?

As they undergo the sorrow of Beethoven's agony,
when pianos have not enough keys to appease
the notes schemed in his inaudible dream.
I'm at the end of me, internally,
as tears, if they could, would see hope fly
from the sights of a lowly stop sign.
As chance took flight out of a window
from crumbling buildings with twin heights,
only to flap featherless arms
into the high skies of death's demise.

I know tears don't do these things;
they don't speak or feel, nor do they have eyes.
They only reflect the unbridled pain
I struggle to bench press inside.
How much of a burden am I supposed to bear
when my heart is aching and my mind doesn't care?
How do I push aside the burden of the world
and convince myself that there be
no greater suffering than mine?
Until then, I'm stuck, holding up
a world I can't change, pretending to be strong
when all I'm brave enough to do is cry.

The Return: Round Trip

I've been here before
stained by the aroma of regrets attached
to insincere apologies...
I return this time tearless, a stark contrast to being fearless
after lying curled up in a pile of me,
not wanting to go back, but the lives of my children...
Well, they depend on me;
it pains, painstakingly, but being in pain guarantees their future
the catch twenty-two of my regrettable remedy.
A step towards doom, a head of stone in grave matters
compels me to perpetually be entombed.

I continually encourage myself with inaudible eulogies,
yet my soul shrieks a more somber euphony.
I took a chance, giddily; I leaped and pranced silly
laughed and danced only to face life sentences
in paragraphs of failure,
a life compiled in misfortunes literary.

I'm back again, burdened to the utmost,
committed to suffering without a future of hope.
Beaten by life, mistakes and flaws
overrun by the reality that I've lost it all
then I look at them, my babies,
a worthy cause to sacrifice for,
live a life in fire for and the reason why I'd break every law.
My fog, the reason to continue
being around when Love becomes wicked–
I think of my babies...
my return tickets.

Don't Breathe

don't do it! hold it in!
don't breathe! just don't breathe!
we got this!
you're breathing again.
please don't do it, ok
just don't do it.

you'll cry, little dove, you'll cry.
they'll know you're not alright, little love. don't cry.
It's only a little lie. we're not okay,
but we're going to be.
that's what we tell them
and bookmark the answer into our little fantasy.
they can't know. it can't show.
but it must go on; that's what they say.
just another moment. it's almost a done day.

(just stop being selfish.
it'll ruin everything he's worked for
and, after all, it's not about us
or what we want.)

What do we want? Don't worry about that;
you gave up individual wants for the sake of the family.

Okay, let's do this. The family needs us. He needs us.
This is our sacrifice. I gave up my life and my wants
for moments like this, for better or worse.
even when love departs, we love until the hearse.

(that's it, distract yourself. just don't breathe.
you're his prize, little dove. you're his prize.
wipe your eyes, little dove. wipe your eyes.
it's only a little lie, little dove. it's alright)

Crack a smile, little dove. Crack a smile.
Remember, it's a lie, little dove. It's a lie.
And if you never cry, little dove,
you'll never need to wipe your eyes.
Just don't breathe. We don't know what truth
may squeak out with that burdensome release.

What is Fear? (IV)

Did you really want
what you said you wanted?
Do you want for fun,
and only need when it's too late?
Do you mentally window shop,
because the fantasy of what you want
is greater than the reality?
Which is the greatest:
having the fear
(you) maintain over yourself as you fail,
or failing because the fear of being successful
is just as hard as the mental journal
of failures you keep?
Do you matter enough to you
to put yourself on the line for your own sake?
Are you comfortable being uncomfortable?
Are you happy being unable
and incapable of being unable for life?
Are you so high on dreams of success
you continually dream to feel better?
Are you a capable dream chaser
relegated to the abysmality of ineptitude?
What is your fear?

THE LIE

which one am I telling?
which truth am I hiding?
which turmoil am I fighting?
your guess. I'm game.
isn't the deception exciting?
wait 'til you hear the truth;
I promise you, it's frightening.

you won't want to hear it
nor come near it
I promise, it's a demiser
whether you know or are none the wiser.
it's catastrophic, hyper-toxic
soul-stealing, life-demeaning
horror-yielding, guilty-feeling
life-fleeting, sorrow-repeating ...

Can you guess? Take your best?
does this look, look true?
is it how I feel?
is it about me? Does it concern you?
trust me when I say don't trust me.
did you trust? haven't you learned?
when the fire sears, it can't be unburnt.

have you found the lie?
have you seen the discrepancies?
could you spot the truth?
there are spaces there.
am I lying through my tooth?

which one am I telling?
which truth am I hiding?
which turmoil am I fighting?
your guess. I'm game.
isn't the deception exciting?
wait 'til you hear the truth.
I promise you, it's frightening.
but until you do,
I guess I'll be practicing another day.

The Snitch

You're always telling:
telling everyone to come and see
Yelling, yelling and yelling
to make everything about me

every time I try to sit, I wince;
make up on, I squint. But here you go
saying come and see the spectacle of embarrassment
that is all of me.

Love covers a multitude,
but makeup covers the devastations of my pulchritude;
mascara masks errors from mass terrors
far greater than forgiveness ever could.

Come and see,
how eye was never the intended target
but it became the bullseye after the fact.
Blows rang then ran rings
around my socket, power connected,
now the greater mark got smaller
and it got down to the pupil

they will see
and you'll tell on him and what he's done,
then another investigation will have begun.
Come and see: the wreck that's been done to me.
Behold how silence bears witness to my loyalty,
simultaneously giving credence to my insanity.

Come and see how marks made
created watermarks where my insecurities
loiter in an amusement park,
a play thing. At least he's entertained
by his affliction of inflicting my pain.
Tattoos of the bruised
marks by hand on hand,
a bloody henna-sullied and soiled,
bullied then spoiled; come and see.
See? He really loves me.

SHADES AND THE BEACH

I took it off, washed all the evidence
that could cause worry or concern.
hung it out to dry, my skin
and the regret that's been tiled within,
hope for a linchpin:
the usually busted lip, fractured ribs
and black eyes.
washed off as much as I could
in hopes of healing faster.
I put it all to the side,
cries followed by deep sigh,
and letting bygones just go on by.

I meander to the beach
to lie in the shade,
for there it cools
all of it
and I pretend to be
free of burden
strife and necessity;
only thing required is that
I be all things necessary ...
necessary for life
necessary for me
necessary for us
necessary for love
just necessary...
temporarily.

Lying on the sand
being held up by something that contours to me, finally
something that's affected by me,
my steps leave imprints.
When I sit, I leave an imprint
I sip my wine and forget things– like how
your fists form, then leave imprints
I breathe and feel the twinge
they feel as though they're conversing...

Maybe reminiscing- (I wish they didn't)
pain happy to see other synapses in like manner
our journey together has brought us this far
to where I feel lost on purpose
unable to make any imprint on your heart.
Ask me how I came to this conclusion
I sip and I regret things.

Pandora's Playlist

Open and unleashed, destruction serenades:
catastrophes peak and peril sounds off
with the magnanimity
of Big Bang grenades adversity creates.
Good fortune decays, beats off the depraved
seeking comfort within the scores of notes,
God conducting the disarray, caught in the fray,
hearts gripped, and then sways.
I faint mid-dismay, too discombobulated to pray.

Here is anguish on display, and music just plays.
Handpicked alphabets, ridiculing Handel's masterpiece.
Angels playing chess with their musicianship, they,
in one accord, tune up my discord.
The soundtrack of my life, baritones of blatancy
running rampant as judgement is rife.
The tumult grows, sour notes implode a
s arteries flattering cello strings begin
to get into the full swing of things.
The crescendo is summoned, misery and malady
being outdone by clanging euphony
and pandemonium's harmony.

Pandora's playlist: she devours and she entreats,
lulling me into disguised peace where I will likely sleep.
She increases pain while I relive shame. Pandora,
what have I uncovered and released?
I'm boxed in, while calamity has cornered me,
still boxing, dodging jeopardy and vulnerability...
a fetish with boxes and jars. Seeing danger afar,
still clinging to hope while Hades' Pied Pipers
cajole me closer to the precipice of apocalypse... deep breaths.
Music stops. Get up to maybe be hurt again.
Pandora's Box unleashed, Pandora's playlist appeased,
wounds haven't yet healed. Traitors haven't made amends.
Music sometimes alleviates the agony
when betrayed by lovers and friends.

WHAT IS FEAR? (V)

How often do you restart
and reengage your dreams?
How many times have you mustered
the courage, only for it to subside
into the mental waste basket
of potential manifestation?
Why are you in limbo, being beaten
by the rod of your own insecurity,
As opposed to rising above it?
How much lower will you sink?
How much longer will you back down
while looking up at what you could be
whether it be happy, content or safe?
How often will you stare into a better tomorrow
while cowering under the frays of yesterday?
Will you hope to death
and have that be your only success?

Why do you still fear?

I Should've

Truthfully, I never envisioned things would end this way.
For the life of me,
I never thought it'd be him, let alone be me.
As a matter of fact, it never crossed my mind
that it would be us.
I never saw the symptoms as profoundly as I felt them.
Foolishly, I never sought after a cure
because the morphine of hope soothed me too much
to look for the cause of the issues, and there were myriads.
I think deep down I always felt like I was the problem
and if I only did right by him,
he'd eventually do right ... by us, hell by me.

Thinking back, I should've said something,
a million times over, I could've said anything.
Maybe how I felt and how it hurt
or how much I'd lost hope in who we used to be.
As mother and wife, I was a great multitasker,
but no matter how good I thought I was,
I was never able to juggle the pain
from the disappointments or the lifestyle,
not to mention our fights.
I was never able to do what was right for myself.

I should've said more than the pain-induced
onomatopoeias that translated my many regrets.
I can't count the occasions I laid lifeless on the floor begrudging
any reason to once again find a purpose for breaths.
I could've left a thousand times over;
I could've fought back. Hell, I could've not settled.
I could have chosen to not see the potential of awesome
that he could've been, but never was.

It is with a heavy heart that I leave with you
these simple gems that I felt were too gaudy for my taste.
My most prized pearls which I never got to wear,
though many occasions swung by.
They are: "I could've, I should've. I didn't... but you can."
Wear them, better than I could've ever imagined.

Must We?

Must we not complain
while in anguish? Refrain from speaking
on the names which brought harm and change?

Must we be metaphorical mute buttons
poked and prodded at will
'til we become discarded pieces,
pretty but valued less than farming feces
to the man you're protecting?
Must we be slaves to their misdeeds,

then found guilty when we choose to be freed?
Is it because our healing affects
your income and your legacy?

Must we, the silenced choir, suffer internally
or eternally in silence while
your success compels our compliance?
Must we base our words and our worth
on the worth of your words as we are
made to look as though
we deserved what occurred?

Must we be silent?
Must we be compliant?
Aren't we?
Must we forgive and forget?
Must we accept that we've become
the successful unsuccessful project?
Must we no longer be
the person we were raised to be,
simply because you were horny
and our presence was convenient?

My fellow victims, we must not. EVER.
You are not alone. We are together.
Culprits like misery, loves company.

Do Not, I Beg You.

Do not commit our sins, nor should you hide
how we shamed and neglected you.
Never forget the agony of our words,
nor the suffering of our abuse.
Run from the injuries of compromise;
these wounds are produced when you've succumbed
to the use of mental crutches, accepting them as normal.
Avoid these kinds of agreements; these are called an internal truce.
Do not hide these scars, for they might
crucify you and haunt your children.
They might pierce your spirit and maim your being,
even with the pain, do not make the mistakes
of staying and merely praying to redundance,
all while being undone, transforming into a shell
of anything you dreamt you'd become.
Karma is Life's bank account,

your misdeeds are its greatest currency.
Do not, I beg you finance the checks of ignorance
by letting rebellion be the expenses
on your soul's bank statements.
We were not perfect; we didn't know any other way,
but we prayed for better days.
Do not add our inconvenience to an already tainted legacy.
Break the cycle and do not complete the circle of calamities.

I beg you!

Do not commit the soul-ending atrocities of complacency
sold to you by patriarchal laws for normalcy.
I beg you, do not!
Instead, stoke the fire of anarchy.
Step boldly on the path to be free,
free to do all things men do, womanly;
be the sum totality of all things necessary,
since all things of necessity find their origin in you.

I beg you not to create walls
so impenetrable that their upkeep
is replete with obituaries of life's defeat.
You are not your ancestors, yet you are.
You are not their mistakes, nor is your life their retake.
You should be the only person living through you.
I beg you not to forgive, only to relive,
nightmares of harm being done to you.
I pray your defaults are filled with responses of love
and not shadowboxing techniques.

I pray your voice becomes a lighthouse
for being unique, and being yourself is axiomatic when you speak.
I beg you not to dim your light nor your mind.
I beg you not to shrink before destiny; every moment is your time.
I beg you, be brave despite the urge to remain scared,
frozen in fear, while the aroma of insecurity refreshes the air.
I beg of you to demand more of yourself than someone else can.
Always see more beauty in your flaws
and the purpose that you flaunt.
I beg you to never beg anyone permission
for being, however you are, in whatever state.
You are universe. You are wombman
in control of your own fate.

Repeatedly (heal, love, breathe)
evolve, live, be (eternally)

WELCOME TO
GRAMMERLIN SQUARE

HOME OF
THE GRANDMENTALSTATION

ALL ABOARD
THE GRANDSCENDENCE

NEXT STOP:

THE PAIN OF A MAN

it seethes, amidst a bevy of unbearables...
fermenting in agony, it smarts, numbing all intelligibility,
making desperate and disconsolate,
it creeps slowly through the mind, making ill the divine
it coaxes, continually baptising rationality into irrational reasoning;
it cooks, after being brought to a slow boil, marinating unawares,
silenced triggers partnered with suppressed shooting,
duality present, a shot in angst from the shooting up of trauma.

This pain devolutionises, riddles and confuses.
Do you feel it, creeping and attacking wholesomeness at whim,
contouring common sense at will?
It injures and maims; this pain stirs disdain
with an inglorious refrain.
The pain of a man is his greatest upkeep,
whether to indulge or keep at bay, to give in
lights the path for decay, and to swim
unlocks all the horrors that have been hid.
The tragedy within a sequence of maladies
all painted with smiles and overt disguises of wellbeing.
The flummery of it all ... depression tiled by smiles,
while insides bawl and the exterior dies.
The poetry of a teary demise.

This pain, twinges on the doorpost of agony
where it hinges in a body swaddled by unwanted memories
becomes motion pictures; the anguish singes, pinges and pangs.
This pain, incapable of being translatable,
still conjugates to travail the uphill battle
to conquer what fully lords over you.
A petition in anguish has now become a law unto you.
This burden accompanied by these wounds that torture,
canst thou describe the metaphysical painkillers
one's soul should prescribe?
This pain blooming with misery and despair
while all else fails; freedom pales while distress reigns.

There is no cure for hope to explore—
just the masterpiece of agony raining
anti-hallelujahs within its karmic symphony.
It seethes ... this pain breathes when you exhale,
it writhes in sorrow and cuts its teeth with grief.
It frees its host into a prison of one, into the great beyond
beneath the substratum of all that is abysmal.
This pain, both Jekyll and Hyde, chides and snides;
it empowers itself to its host's dismay
and leaves a microcosmic wreck from its emotional hurricane.

.

This pain plays defense under unassuming pretence;
it never relents, interchanging discontent with malcontent,
spiralling as it disorients into an unfathomable descent.
How will you overcome after the Groundhog Day replays of being undone,
the resilient crescendo is a silent swan song of oblivion.
This pain feels then makes numb; this pain sees then makes blind.
It disrupts while it corrupts, it grows as you fade.
emotionally spayed, mentally frayed.
We are they that decayed before they decay.

This pain... is.

Wyatt P. Riverledge

Born into no great house;
no form of nobility was attributed to me..
There is no divine skill that I can exclusively lay claim to;
no sense of infamy or popularity, cept of the transient kind
that is up until recently. You see I am a bard
(though I utterly loathe that word)
this is why by my own standards, I am a painter of history.
I may not be the first to tell it, but I am able to add a fresher,
more entertaining coat after a time, especially
to where no "paint" has been applied. For some time I've travelled across
various lands telling exaggerated and sensational version of several
widely known stories. Why you may ask- the answer is simple my tales
in spite of their historical accuracy don't
get much attention like they used to, and since my livelihood depends
on my storytelling- I've decided to add more than my fair share of variety
to try and spice things up. Truth is whenever I begin to embellish,
I become so obsessed by the cheers and the applause; I spose,
I've become rather fond of their laughter and amazement,
even if by the end of a fortnight I shan't be remembered...
because I always remember.

But if I may be honest, lately, I've been passably bored;
thoughts of posterity and legacy have had my thoughts quite occupied.
I needed something fresh and unusual- a story that the masses
don't know or haven't heard before. What could it be and how
would I come up with it? This I did not know, but I was desperate
even if it meant violating whatever morals I had left.
While stewing in this slumpful and dejected state,
it was time for me to be travelling to a new city;
as Id already gotten the most of this unpainted town, it was time to go.
Maybe the change of scenery will inspire me or perhaps
the gods will bestow some semblance of favour upon me.
Something had to happen, sooner or later.

I've always liked the prospect of travelling, because unfamiliar cities
brings forth fresh ears, more chances to further enhance signature stories,
they also allow a more affordable livelihood. While on this trip,
I was out of sorts with no wherewithal to pay for much of anything.
This isn't unusual, for to be a travelling painter of times it was more important
to look the part, than actually doing so- one attracts a more favourable amount of
fortune compared to those that appear miserly. I do spose there's
a bit of illogic at best, but it works and has always worked,
no one had been successful otherwise
so there was no genuine incentive to be antithetical.

Upon my arrival, I had nowhere to stay, nor did I have anything to eat.
knowing this, I took to a leisurely stroll around the community,
greeting each person I passed by or came in contact with

all while showcasing my singing ability of course- this is all
part of my prep for the show I intended to perform when the time was right.
Somehow during the time spent meandering about- I got lost and stumbled
upon an old and what looked like an abandoned cabin. Wretched thing,
dilapidated and unkempt; desperate for a place to stay,
humble pie would be my first meal here it would seem.
I patrolled the area to see if anyone would lay claim,
maybe some scullion or vagabond
maybe someone in a position such as myself,
you know out sorts and so on. after some time,
no one came to the deserted abode
so I took liberty in calling it home until I came into some good fortune.

While seeking if the cabin had a comfortable place
to sleep or maybe even water to take a bath
I tripped over some old manuscripts. they had no names to identify
an author, just a few faded stories about civilizations of old.
I couldn't use these in my stories, that era and the current times
we were in had nothing in common, but it was so intriguing and captivating.
I mulled and mused, all night trying to find something or some way to use them.
I was clueless and enthralled I just knew within my core
that it was important to tell these stories or share them at the very least.

These stories tell of how things came to be, how those niggers
came to be lower than livestock. it showed a strategic plan
of how to overcome generational slavery. it showed a people willing
to take destiny by any means and overturn the tyranny of those godawful niggeries.
What deity could be so base as to allow livestock to have reign, let alone freewill.
I was appalled, I couldn't believe what I saw, what I read
even with the preposterous lines, it was captivating. the intellect,
the willpower that it took for them to overcome; I thought to myself,
this must be shared. the world must know about such brilliant
and well laid plans for us to remain in power.

I thought of the best ways to have these manuscripts stay in my possession.
who hid them? why did they hide them? how did they come to be here?
Am I being watched? I immediately feared for my safety
and packed my things and left immediately.
I didn't know where these writings would take me,
I knew I had to get away. So I did, reading and rewriting as best as I could.
making it a more plausible story that of the like of David and Goliath.
it took me years to share these stories over the years;
hoping its true author would begin to tell the story.
To this day no one has told a story even close
to that which has been in my possession.
I look around, becoming uncomfortable with the befriending
of these discardables and it upsets me.
so I have chosen to set forth these manuscripts as my own
in hopes of us uniting as the forefathers did when
they conquered these maroon savages.

what you are about to read, in these manuscripts
are pertinent for the maintenance of our survival;
in order for us to keep control we must revert
to the ways of the first fathers
and renounce the alliances we have forged
for sake of business and commerce.
also that which I'm about to share are the seeds of the trees
that would have us see no lack from now 'til judgment come.
Pray it doesn't- ever in the name of their beloved deities and orishas
and gods and whoever else they believe in.
Down with the niggers and all that they bring.
Down with their black skin and ungodly pronounced features.
I hope with thorough sincerity that these manuscripts pave
the way for us to in full control again; 'til time ceases.

This is the Inception.

Wyatt Pierre-Paul Riverledge

Inception: The Crescendo

At the peak of riches and comfort.
Well-fed and satiated by the many victories
from conquests- for once all tribes, nations, villages and provinces
were united mainly by business and barter. Peace and overflow
was rife along the Mother continent. There prestige and wealth seeking
dampened and dulled their warrior spirit. the many voices of praise overtook
the one of their ancestors. ego became their sun and pride became their moon.
success reigned and where there was once a strong and powerful bond
between a land and its people - there's is now an egregious disconnect
and no one saw a better a time to pounce than their servants
who never knew power or wealth of their own.

They grew envious and jealous,
wanting to partake in the joy and revelry
unable to while seeing their abject
poverty and legacy of children starve and suffer
they now had a mutual goal- for the first time ever
for mutuality evaded them forever
except in complexion and status, so they united- putting aside
petty differences trying to see how to overtake or overcome.
They tossed aside, reasons for wars and the petty bickering
about lifestyles and life choices, did away with family grudges
and pointless stalemates between parents long gone once and for all,
because the chance to change the alignment of the stars of their destiny
was before them and more possible than ever.

they knew the gathering and dissemination of intelligence was a factor
or as they called it- knowledge filtering. They're masters controlled
the possession and flow of information along with the wealth- so if there
was a lack of information they were able to correct it with money.
The plight of the slaves was dire- their need great and their task
indubitably unsurmountable. They knew proper plans were needed
because protesting didn't work anymore- complaining wasn't enough
crying dried quicker than the blood of their martyrs. they became numb
heartless and recalcitrant- burdened and tired. going through
the processes of routine killings and their inability
to exact revenge or achieve justice.

Their protests became silent and secretive, trained and tactical
so much so that their behaviour went unnoticed to their masters
who grew more unaware as they grew comfortable.
their ancestors were chanting for change and for them to be woke
but they celebrate their fattened state- deaf to warnings
ignoring the imploring- starving their responsibility
and wasting their legacy by feeding their iniquities.
so their slaves plotted- making headway by tasking
the pre-eminent slaves to mark down anything and everything of note;
their routines, their true weakness and honest and planned responses.

the chief of these Adam- who was the first of our kind
to be as trusted as he was. he was a beautiful soul,
and well beloved by all of them
he was their betrayer.
he was our task manager, the very last of us
who eventually grew tired of his teacher
and mentors hurting his people
their intellectuality waned their prowess
and hunger for progress died with them.
the honour of being premiere lost its lustre
and being that he was of no threat to them.
they taught him everything- to fight like them,
think like them
and how to manoeuvre against them.
They spoke strategies and how they could be defeated
and he was privy to all of it.
He was our leader- because they'd never expect it from him.
This was our rebellion, our insurrection.
This is our inception.

Inception- The Beginning

secret sign for a meeting is shown
the slaves gather follow the determinded routes
and actions of protocol for the gathering.

Adam: the leaders are
at their mandatory prayer ceremony
thanking their ancients.

voice: their ancients, no doubt.
murmuring and mumbling.

Adam: truly, their ancients.

voice: when do we begin conquering?
agree, when do we begin! tell us, because you know.

Adam: It is not merely a matter of conquering
but a question of maintaining.
I'm sure we're all aware acquisition is easy,
but maintaining, well that's a gift to accomplish.
so I ask how do we maintain?

voice: well we conquer and destroy them, no?

voice: and then after we destroy them we all would start afresh?

voice: but what happens if we all start from the same place
as them after the destruction?

Adam smiling because he knows what needs to be done.

Cain: we need a head start because if we were to start equally
they'd have us beat 9 times out of ten
and we don't know for sure if that tenth time will come.
you see how long we waited for this tenth time

Adam: I like that idea- what would be better
is if we had a series of headstarts.

Cain: Right, headstarts that lead into other headstarts,
kinds that starts at every junction possible
for the best form of continuity possible.

voice: I understand the headstarts
but how do we prevent them from benefitting from the headstarts

Adam: we make certain advantageous requirements,
for instance— the kind that only reflect our successes
and compounds the headstarts we've taken.

voice: I like that- so if they don't look like us they get denied or delayed...

Cain: these are all very good ideas- do we have anymore

voice: what do we do in case they procreate?
Do we kill them? if so,
how do we do this without violating our beliefs.

Cain: very good question

Adam: anyone? better yet
I have this one- if we manipulate the environment
and make it conducive to their abject failure;
we do this for both parent and offspring who will be regulated,
which includes their birthing, living and their dying.
now that I think about it, their failure has to work part and parcel
with each headstart we designate. if we can rid them of what they believe
is core to their beliefs, integral to their hope, taint their beliefs,
and toggle with their nutrition thereby reducing their form of living
at least three times beneath what we have and a half a level above poverty.

Cain: why would we do all of that?

Adam: they'll be too focused on living -
while running away from not dying to focus too much on us
and if they ever get close we squeeze their options
bring them closer to death- or bribe them to betray their cause
by elevating their status and income.

voice: do you really think, that'll work.

Adam: with more planning
yes especially if we devastate
their normalcies and make them desperate.
feeding a broken chicken is subservient 'til he heals.
it must remain broken at all costs. Any more ideas?

Cain: yes, we could put together a system of laws
that would further handicap them not to mention
compliment and supplement all the various headstarts
that we would put into play.
Not too blatant to be easily believed
and not to subtle that it's not possible
but governed enough to where it's not provable

voice: what we need is to build it up to its most complex peak
then create a skeletal version to allow change overtime.

Adam: I like that- so as we progress the most minor alterations
have the most major and significant implications

voice: what would make it more realistic as well perfect,
is if we- every once in a while allow an anomaly
who completely conformed to all the guidelines
we delineated for them to cohabitate with us.
we would need to hound the anomaly into complete conformation
if balanced precisely, it would give off the right amount of hope
because its attainable and the right amount of dissuasion
because they have to go thru an unreal vetting process
and we retain the right to both choose
and regulate the anomaly and their rewards,
after they turn their back on their people.

Adam: brilliant - brilliant- no area must be unaccounted for.
we must remain in control at all times.

Cain: I think we left out a valid point
and that is money, resources, land and information
and technology - things we don't currently monopolize.

voice: how do we do that

Adam: we monopolize these things by learning.
learning how they acquired
and how they were capable of maintaining it
then we systematically cut off all the heads
of all leaders across the board
we begin this phase only after learning from them
what disarms them and lulls them into thinking we care
and when they are comfortable and fat- we strike.

Cain:(How)
Adam: I'm not sure-but while we do this
we have to begin indoctrinating and inculcating
the children on both sides; ours to obscene confidence
that they should be incapable of seeing the truth
and theirs to always see the truth
but rarely see it manifest in their favour,
no matter how blatantly obvious
we must miss it while they can't help but see it.
enough for today, we reconvene at a later date

Inception: The Execution

voice: the leaders have all turned in
for the night after the wedding of first children.

Adam: now that we've begun to address some of the issues
we could possibly face- is it safe to say that a plan
of action has been decided upon
and how comfortable we are with progress
and process towards our forever future....

voice: yes we have a great start plan somewhat motion
and I speak for all when I say that -
but how and when do we begin?
As of right now we don't have the numbers.

Adam: this is true, it must be said

voice: nor do we have any of the handicaps
or head starts you so eloquently alluded to.

voice: Let's not even talk about the finances,
this has never been done before,
history is not in our favour, nor was it
neither the present- we don't even have the power?
how do we plan such an illustrious future?

voice: I agree, all these years planning- was it all for nought.

voice: what are our chances to be successful. let alone start.

voice: what he's saying is,
we just don't want all our work
and sacrifices to be in vain.
voice: I can speak for myself,
if it is in vain and it is some pipedream,
we should quit while ahead

Adam:(deep sigh)
I understand how you feel.
voice: but do you?

Adam: I too have been impatient
I too have had my share of doubt and dread.
How can I forget the past when my forefathers were the rebel rousers
don't remind me how they were flogged, flayed and crucified.

voice: we're.... (interrupted)

Adam: Don't you dare
I didn't come to you about this, you came to me
do I suffer less because I came from a great name of servants?
no, we all suffer- we all pay from their gluttony,
arrogance and pompous cruelty.
Mine isn't greater than yours
nor is your misery less relevant than mine
but this is why we have these meetings...
to properly address any potential leaks,
weaknesses, or subtle areas of susceptibility.
its better when we come to each other
rather than discussing it publicly where others hear
and attempt to crumble our foundation.

voice: thank you for validating our thoughts
and insecurities, it means the world.

Adam: you are right, but only if we remain united
will we have the world
and then we will have the sun and the moon.

voice: So how do we proceed? How do we begin?

Adam: first things first
do we have all posts accounted for?
are the chosen ones from each family
a servant or student in all
the required locations of future control?

Cain: Yes we have all the *nervously* assassins
in all the homes of all the heads of houses across the lands.
we even have help from some of the scorned among them

voice: interrupts- we even have the help of the sympathizers
who feel they have been stripped, exiled and embarrassed
even those who feel left out of their society.

voice: interrupts- That's really good
they've always wanted change- just too befallen,
misfortunate and abandoned to do anything about it...

Adam: restoring order- I'll say this-
I don't have an issue with them helping
but this must be said- once we've accomplished our goal
they must certainly be among the dead.
a member of a society who betrays his people
by helping outsiders overthrow them is one fault away
from betraying his co-conspirators which we would be.
we may be aligned in our goal
but our reasons and visions are vastly different.
They only seek revenge while we thirst for a future
where we maintain complete and total control.

Cain: It is safe to say that everyone is accounted for
and awaiting further instructions.
what do we do now?

voice: what do we do to prevent them from taking over again.
even with the head starts- even with the handicaps
and advantages we will be putting in place.

voice: Also, remember it was said
that they're stronger,
healthier, better.
what do we do?

Adam: Easy - We go to war

voice: War?

voice: you've got to be kidding!

voice: they'll beat us, so what then

Cain: Easy- we kill them?

voice: What about their allies wont they rise against us,
if they do they'll return and they'll win again
and punish us for the rebellion and we might not be here again.

Adam: (smirks) we kill them all. smartly, secretly and strategically...
we call them our assassins....
(looks around the room)
for a reason and if they are in the places instructed
their allies will also fall thereby making them also helpless.

voice: how do we kill strategically?
does that even make sense?
is this a silent war?

voice: I like that but something else has to happen no?
do we maintain killing them or will something be done to regulate
their lives and livelihood.
something major, tragic;
I think we need to plan this now before
we can begin our plans and maintain our plans.

Adam: we didn't discuss this in full but we alluded to this prior.
I think we should go back to the beginning
and work our way down. simplify it.

voice: ok, lets....

Adam: that's it right there- we have our people who are pupils
of the heads of houses these are also our best assassins.
when we've learned how to acquire
and maintain all things they currently maintain,
mindlessly and meticulously.
we will begin to steal unmissables -
things that don't usually get accounted for.
We'll use these items to lie to their allies
and their enemies to gain their support.
Once we have maintained proper relations
and have gotten more adept at stealing
we will make the necessary moves to kill the heads of houses
everywhere. their people will try to find a culprit
we give them of the ones who aren't with us.
and while they're mourning. we kill them.

Cain: Adam, we could kill the heads of houses, but why stop there?
Why not murder those who would man
and start and lead a successful revenge war against us
if they found out what we did to their masters.
all we'd have to do is leave the least resistant,
least vengeful, most docile, charming
and least military minded to take charge.
Whoever it is they must be a convincingly influential person
who would sacrifice the livelihood of a nation
just to preserve their family.
those- we'd leave in charge under constant threat
of killing their posterity who we'd hold hostage
so they will be forced to convince their nation
who would not only be in shock but duress
they would have to make them very compliant
and cooperative making it easier implement
what we need and make the necessary changes we need.
voice: so we'd kill their heads of houses
just to hold the most coward one in charge?

Adam and Cain: Yes

voice: but what do we do with them?
we've spoken about killing them
we'd need to have control of them
to lord over all of them to systematically, no?

Cain: the best we have always been are farmers.
maybe if we treated them like livestock
taming the alpha to maintain order
we could accomplish all our tasks.

voice: so we cage them?

Cain: cage sounds too inhumane - they're still human

voice: maybe we can change how they're viewed anyway.

Adam: we could use what is familiar to them.

voice: which is what?

Adam: Enslavement?
enslavement allows us to do all of the above we've planned.
they're already familiar with how it works.
all we need to do is make the price of freedom
unrealistically attainable
while they undergo the most brutal barbaric
and cruel forms of treatment
we wouldn't wish on our worst of our people
all while we take their lands,
rename and rework their achievements,
rewire their mindset- and cripple their future.
we could make them build the head starts...
enslavement allows us to establish and negotiate handicaps
from now 'til kingdom come.
if we execute the plan- we execute the people
let those who have been judged- judge.

Let us begin

The Inception.

Inception: Legacy of Families

Adam: I have heard the clamours and the doubts.
I've heard them all and I am disgusted.
We have come too far to be dismantled by doubts of a future so brilliant
and astounding. We will not be swindled by degenerates
that can't see beyond their skintight insecurities.
We will not falter, we will not stumble.
From this day forth we do not do things merely because of tradition.
We do not do things merely because of legacy.

The journey we are about to embark on is greater
than the pathetic and meagre crumbs of history
we've been far too naive to share.
We rewrite history, legacies and norms.
We claim the future as our own
and mould it for our children's children
the ones we won't get to hold.
if these ambitions are too haughty
for you weaklings and coward in hearts.
Depart now and face death or remain and be counted amongst history
when we retell their tales and extraordinary feats.
all things we do from this point forward is out of necessity
not and not ego, anger nor arrogance.
Our subservience must be raised to a higher level
as it continues to keep them unawares.

Anyone willing to leave? Good. it is important that these facts,
plots and schemes remain with us- and to ensure that this is the case -
(all individuals here will take a blood oath - those sworn fealty)
will be given a post to oversee within the areas of control.
it is important to note that what we do now
is for the greater good of our community.
the virtues and principles of righteousness
keeps us docile and in an unimpactful rut.
we eat to live and not to be pleased.
we will marry, not out of love but as a part of our strategy,
empowerment and for us to look united long after we've gone.
in regards to the community,
the individuals in the rooms of every meeting
will take blood oaths to ensure the utmost care
is taken with regards to our progress.
each of us will have areas of control or an area of control.

The control areas will overlap and when they do,
ego must be put aside for the continued survival of our people.
we will setup families to be in control
and if they violate secrets or embarrass us....
they will be extinguished in their entirety.
and the family without am area of control
that is next in line will take over if they choose.

we will always be ready to serve each other -
must be ready to only believe each other and defend each other -
these are our plans- that families will be immovable institutions -
bringing forth a future where we're never undermined
and never out of control-and if anything is loose or missing
we must at all times selflessly address
in all manners whether fixing or admonishing
one another as we focus on each other
no one person will be unaccounted for,
nor can be.
is this understood?

(all say aye)
AYE

INCEPTION: ASSEMBLY LINE

Adam- welcome brothers in strife.
While our wives perform the taxes for the masters,
we have some time to further bolster any plans
or utilise any other ideas that we might
not have thought about initially.

young voice: Lord Adam,
I'm not of any great importance sir
but I have an idea that could help us maintain control.
|You see how we make that chain
when we pass each other food
from the field to the harvest house?
We line up to assemble how we want the room to be efficient for our use.
We children can understand where to put the fruits
the vegetables and the beans.
Can this method help out with the plans for our future?

voice: children should not speak
nor should they be allowed in the room
when discussing matters so grave and pertinent.

Adam: Please hold your tongue.
If you do not understand the brilliance of what was said,
then completely hold your peace.

Adam: little one, you do know what the biggest issue
we have with your aid when given?
Punishing you for your youthful exuberance.
Because of your youth and giddiness,
you're more prone to mistakes.
But because of your youth,
your energy allows you to recover quickly
from the mistakes you made.
Also, because you aren't aware of your mistakes
you leave more of a mess behind.

the room agrees...

Adam: so we are left to make amends,
even after you've felt like you did a great job.
Let this be a lesson to us all. Youthful exuberance is not an excuse
for a poorly done task. This child, has just given us great insight
with how we bring about and maintain the changes we need.
This will also be key in making the headstarts
flow more efficiently and effectively.
Cain: will you explain this to us?

Adam: we use an assembly line concept
where the assembler is free from fault
if the quality of the product is defective.

voice: I don't follow, please explain more of this,
this- assimilly whatever you said.

Cain: mass production

Adam: Yes, mass productions, where we have an assembly line
on every level for every headstart.
Based on our plan for optimal survival and dominance -
how can we get the desired results without being blatantly implicated
or outright guilty. Truth is, there are more fools than avenues of truth,
some will find out but their revelation and their efforts
to make a change won't, nor can it be successful
if our headstarts and handicaps work.

voice: but what is this assembly production line,
it sounds intriguing- subtly deviant

Adam: many hands make the work light, we've heard for a long time.
In an assembly line- it is a column or line or row
of workers who are readying a package or product to be available...
the package is the most subservient, brainless,
docile, yet hard working healthy strong
and powerful sleepwalker, that ever live.

voice: the compliant dead.

Adam: Yes, the hidden secret of leadership
at its paramount is to make the package
think their ideas are theirs
when in truth we control them, down to the times
when they have mustered enough frustration to rebel.
It will serve our purpose.
We have complete control down to the most minuscule minutiae.

voice: so we want to have an assembly line for history,
culture, sports, health and life?

voice: an assembly line for every area of existence.

Cain: we dispatch a house from the LOF
to each assembly line for optimum control.

Adam: we seem united in this.
Are all intentions and requirements clear?

All: Aye

INCEPTION: FARMERS MARKET

Adam: today we speak about maintenance.
We've long been taught by our soon to be former masters
that the acquisition of a thing is cheaper than its upkeep.
When we've conquered them, we need to do our due diligences
to ensure that we maintain an irrepressible stronghold,
through the LOF, the headstarts
and our united duty to our existence.
Full control is what we're aiming for,
a stranglehold of everything down to the minutiae.
There should be no lack or avenue left up to chance.
Nary an area of their life should be left to happenstance,
faith or coincidence.

voice: May I speak?

Adam: please

voice: what are we going to do about their bodies.
All these plans of conquering
and dominance and killing.
But what about their bodies.

voice: their bodies!? What do you mean,
what should we do with their bodies?
What's the purpose of this assembly line
gots to do with their bodies?

Cain: if we don't do something with the bodies,
we'll die from the piles of dead bodies.
So something has to happen
and since we're already talking about a system of killing
to perpetuate our rule for many a millennia to come.
We have to find the most viable way that aligns
with our headstarts to deal with their bodies.

Adam: you reap what you sow.

Cain: harvesting?
Adam: you said they have stronger organs
which are housed in a stronger ecosystem.
If we control their livelihood - we could indirectly farm
and harvest their organs as a way to prolong our life
extending our life ensure our foundational ideas continue
to thrive for as long as we need to implement them into the next in line.

voice: I don't mean to interrupt, but if we're killing them
why not choose when to and how to kill them
so their organs aren't wasted.

Cain: doctors in the room,
what have they taught us in regards to science
where they can die without any major damage taking place?

voice: murder maybe?

Cain: murder raises too much suspicion.

Adam: not if we are the law,
jury and the judge,
which are all housed under the LOF

voices: we agree, right we have that covered
in our head-starts and control towers.

Cain: what about stealing them?

voice: stealing?

voice: yes, talking their children
and putting them to sleep.
So we can preserve the organs before they die.
This will help us prolong life and choose
when we and how we kill them
and last longer as we discussed earlier.

voice: not too young
where they need more development
but old enough where the parts
we need can support an adult body.

Cain: that sounds, ingenious
but how do we do this on a full scale?

Adam: I think it best to create and cultivate
the perfect processes and procedures based,
have these texts hidden under a different name,
that only the LOF can find and understand the text.

voice: genius

Cain: truthfully, we need their dead bodies for practice,
considering we desire study their anatomy that we can learn
how to best harvest their organs.

Adam: we also need to create harvest stations across
every land we inhabit so we can use the best methods to harvest organs.
And close locations to aid in the kidnapping of their legacy.

Cain: the harvest stations can go hand in hand with the headstarts

voice: we can disguise the stations as hospitals
where behind closed doors we can manoeuvre
as freely as we would like or need.

Cain: what does that mean?

Adam: it means everyone is allowed to come,
but we only cure our own
and use the sick station as a place to swap,
harvest or infect as needed.

voice: clean thieves...
voice: why not just call it harvesting and farming.
We turn them into crops, we've been doing it for ages now.

Adam: the hospital will be a farmers market
for all our life extending needs.

Cain: the time for this meeting is almost up-
what have we decided upon in short

Adam: we need to create harvest stations -
hospitals that are equipped to withstand all temperatures.
We need methods that we can improve on over time
that will allow us to safely and securely remove body parts
which can be used at a future time.
So the most prominent of us during those eras
can continue our work for as long as they can.
This plan will be called the farmers market.
'til next time- be safe and be secretive.

Inception: Creating Ghosts

Adam: It is with a stern disposition
that I propose a bulletproof form of action to absolve ourselves
as a whole unit from any guilt that could at some point implicate us
in the foreseeable and the unforeseeable future.

voice: that sounds good, we would now have protection
with what's coming and after it happens.

voice: it does sound like the insurance plan we need.
In addition to all the other plans we have been preparing,
but how can we do that? It seems a tall task for what we want to achieve?
Do we need to do this?

Cain: would you want your grandchildren or great grandchildren
in a room similar to this decrying our inability
to maintain what we've here and now started?

voice: you do have a point. But how do we so this?

Adam: there's no easy way to say this
but we create ghosts
we need to create absurdly yet strategically elaborate ghosts
(loud laughter- obscene laughter)

(attempting to stop the laughter for himself
and others so his point can be heard).

voice: are we really talking about ghosts?
After all that we've planned for? Ghosts?
Elaborate? You are correct, absurd is the best word
you can you to surmise such an imbecilic plot.
We have enough strategy to last us a few generations.
We don't need any more schemes,
let alone ridiculous plans about ghosts.

snickering

voice: do you have any idea what you're saying? Have you lost it?
A few of us think you've gone over the edge
and are in no way shape fit to continue as our leader.

Adam: I see, and this feeling is mutual around the room is I assume.

scattered voices: it is- tis so- here here

Adam: so are we saying - I should bequeath my position as visionary
and that I should step down? Hand over the keys so to speak.

voices: yes - no (more nays than yays)

voice: if I may, no one is saying that you should step down
(looks around) at least not all of us.
We just don't know anything about ghosts.
The myths and legends of their ancestors
rest heavier with you than us,
we understand this is because of your proximity.
It's always been their thing to deal with spirits and so on -
why would we need to do it?
Bear in mind we know not the purpose
it'll serve now or for the future.

Adam: I can understand, from the looks of it,
that it would seem problematic to present an idea about ghosts.
I understand completely. But if anyone were to find out
the details of these meetings, our families would suffer mercilessly.
I'm merely proposing a means by which
we wouldn't be held accountable for anything at all.
I know we don't believe in ghosts, but we can manufacture
an idea of them to help absolve ourselves as a whole unit
from any guilt that could at some point implicate us.
We need to create absurdly elaborate ghosts
whose existence to the T has been perfectly concocted
for anyone to deny that they existed. It must be said once again,
it must be a popular name, from a common street;
we must recycle the names as they do after their ancestors
so as to ensure this plan goes through ad seamlessly as possible.
I think it is ingenious if our guilt is transformed into a straw-man
whose existence is actual but unprovable
this may help us in more ways than one in the coming generations.
No matter how much they try to blame a person,
the systems are at fault- and the leader in charge
will always be the target of their hate their angst and their turmoil.
He will be tasked with the burden of carrying on our legacy to the fullest.

voice: I see- when you say ghost you mean an allegorical scapegoat
to which we all would wear the mask in unison.
We'd be guilty but the arguments they'd bring against us
wouldn't even be against us directly.
It'd be against the system we've put in place
and we wouldn't be around for that by the time they would blame us.

Adam: exactly, they would blame us eventually then continually.
But our children are not us, they will be guilty by virtue of posterity,
legacy and tradition; but as we've discussed
if we execute this plan well enough
it'd be so second nature to continue
that our offspring wouldn't even be aware consciously
except those of the LOF.

voice: this is ingenious. Wow- we've come a long way.

voice: truly a long to be able to devise a plan such as this
and I pray your health and strength that we all
can and will be seeing it all the way through.

Cain: I'm speechless. Incredible.

Adam: this allows us to be as ruthless and vengeful, merciless
and callous for the years we've been subservient and docile.
Mere afterthoughts and less than human,
this is for everybody that got flogged,
tortured by their barbarism and their cruelty.
We will rewrite their history and their glory as our own.
We will deceive their generation
of all their goodness and marvellous feats.
Everyone won't believe, but the majority will
and we will pound them over and over,
inculcating and imbibing them
into perfect little byproducts of frustrated obedience.
Where they'll be forced to choose to be troubles by the times
or die trying to make a dent into the series of systems.
I ask, now... are hearts and mind clear?
Do I need to step down?

All: Minds and hearts cleared.
All that is, should remain the same.

Voices: Reign Adam Reign.

Wyatt P. Riverledge

In my naive exuberance,
I was willing to share all of my manuscripts.
I am not as young as I used to be
nor have I lived the lavish life of my heyday,
this is in essence a last ditch effort for world renown.
After seeing the clamour and excitement,
I have chosen to release them in a timely fashion.
With no explanation,
I place the onus solely on you to figure out the timeline.
They will not be accompanied by any sort of commentary,
and the releases will be sporadic and random.
I hope this will be as eye opening for you as it was for me.
'Til I share with you again. this is where we must part.

Wyatt Pierre-Paul Riverledge

My Children

Our children, we failed you
in taking our future for granted,
and it doomed us all.
We forsook the lessons of our ancestors
while we taught the outsiders everything
and what we showed them,
they took, then used against us ...
leaving us with nothing.
We lament what has happened
we didn't see it coming
we do not know how it happened
nor do we know how to regain
what we lost ... that is, all of you.

We beg you forgive our failures, our failings
for we have tried;
however, there are some amongst us
who, in secret, constantly conspired to betray us.
We have not lost hope,
but we have no clue
how to now find the culprits responsible.

Over time we eventually knew,
because the poorest of us
had things neither
they nor their ancestors had before.
So we addressed them,
and our little ones were taken
and assaulted before our eyes.
The anger of ancients consumed us
so we set out for them,
but they sought refuge
from the wealthy among us,
who for the sake of losing their families
and wealth conspired with the foreigners.
We pray to the ancestors
every day for your return;
we pray for your safety.

We pray you haven't forgotten us.
We hope you learned
the lessons we failed to teach.
We hope you'll be better versions
of what we appeared to be ...
better versions of all
the unfavourable unsavoury images
that have stained your memories.

We wonder how many of our teachings
stayed with you, or will stay with you.
We wonder how many of our blueprints
remain with you.
We wonder if you'll commit the same wrongs;
we wonder if we did enough,
completely convinced we could've done more.
We just don't know where or how.

We thought we did a good job with what we knew;
we didn't know enough as we brought shame to you.
To our ancestors, you were our greatest wealth.
Now we wonder how much of our wealth
was squandered because we never knew
what made us wealthy.

My children, we wonder
if you'll remember us in the good times
and not the times we face now?
I wonder if our children will ever meet your children?
I wonder if we'll build a new world
together one day, or will we be divided forever
from the last time we saw each other?

Our children, we are crying
while your screams mute our lamentations.
We struggle daily, trying not to forget
your faces or your sounds of laughter.
We struggle with losing our kin
as our greatest mistakes.
We pray that we'll meet our ancestors- you and us
another time, in a much better place.

GENEXODUS I

"Grammah, can you tell us a story"
Grammah: unnuh wah mi tell a story?
Well com siddung mek mi tell unnuh one den!

who will take away the pain
who will make it go away
tell us who
tell us who
who will give us our just due?
If not us, then why not you?

We cried, desperately crying away our pain
in songs about anything, anything that will rid of us
of the overwhelming resentment within.
So we sing with agonising melodies
so heart-wrenching that angels lose wings
trying to petition the mercy of God to hear our cries.

He always fails to answer, so hope has died
in our minds and before our eyes;
each and every time, our skin explodes
when it crashes against the master's leather.
The very same whip, designed with bones and nails,
that repeatedly greets us with torrential thrashings
'til our mangled bodies perfectly
reflect the stormy weather ...
Can I tell you a story?

THE BLOOD REMEMBERS

Waking up to heart-racing cold sweats,
reliving history like I was there.
All images clear except the finale.
On the brink of death 'til consciousness reappears.
It remembers the beauty of the land and the harvest therewith;
it remembers the livelihood of the people
and how they danced and cheered.
I remember, faintly, the blood isn't as strong as it once was.
But it remembers in part...

The diadem of space, the earth and all therein.
We were all things by becoming everything
in a world where no progress was withheld from us
in any way, shape, or form.
We learned and taught to our hearts' desire;
we loved and forgave 'til our naïveté brought us to a ship.
After being betrayed, we were dragged aboard
or met our ancestors in their celestial grave.
It remembers, the blood now faint,
but after I awake, it's never the same.

I remember a life I never lived,
saw the days I took breaths surrounded by people
who didn't look like the individuals I called family.
I was elevated to heights I'd never seen,
taken aback while being taking back, with my eyes closed.
This is the only dream that I see before they open again,
and therewith did I last breathe.
I remember how the view of trees
that swung in the breeze as they swayed. So did eye.
One with Mother Nature moving in harmony.
I, in death, as she bore life,
I closed my eyes and every day since, I can remember.
History reminding me about the lives of my ancestors died on a tree.

I wake up in cold sweats, screaming out from my worst fears.
I'm trapped because I tapped in to the inner me,
which seemed like betrayal to the enemy
who seeks my end to continue his reign in tyranny.
I was running from police dogs
after they blasted me with the water hose.
I'm running for my entire life, dodging every obstacle
hat looks innocent, avoiding gunshots and dog bites.
I'm frightened and at my wit's end, a body dogged and run ragged
by rabid dogs whose speed I can no longer contend with.
Running still, crying aloud, running past signs
where no niggers are allowed,
and there where I always wake. I fell.

Cotton Porn

(Sing)

"Bring a wagon and all your pence,
new niggers have arrived.
Dress them good and proper
to catch a buyer's eye.
Break them in and teach 'em;
a good nigger abides
and if the wretch should run away,
beat them till they bleed,
then hang the niggers dry."

They get off on it:
these good and godly Christian folk
who live free off of the work for which we bleed,
and unleash their cruelties while telling us
to trust and obey then hope and pray
that one day we'll be Christians worth saving
if we remain docile in their shackles of slavery.
We were chained and He was chained.
They, the Romans and we like their Christ,
but it's not the part of the story they like.
So we pick cotton all day in the fields,
bludgeoned and whipped,
whimpering with staggered steps.
They got off on us while we got off cotton,
picking bloody dreams.
See, we dreamt of home like their Elysian Fields.

'til them whips changed the address.
We was here now, walking down
rows of white with burdens laden,
walking between whites with hands and feet of red.
Sun kissed and blood drenched,
body whipped and wounds fresh.
They'd tell you god and all
them angels was blinding white,
but we the ones being pierced, holey and living right.
The ones who was betrayed and being crucified,
we the ones giving our lives, bearing their sins
dying to accommodate their Phariseesistic lifestyle.
We walked within them white lines,
the ones with cotton and the ones they made up.

They got off on us, we were born as super heroes
with Caucasian insecurities as our kryptonite;
black men and women were of stronger cotton,
picked on then picked off faster than a two-faced Uncle Tom.
Our ancestors hung 'til they went hanging with their ancestors.
They got off of us, while we sang negro spirituals;
seeking new methods of dominance was their daily ritual.
White, addicted to black trauma and negro pain,
these godly Christians, who believed their deeds
would entice Jesus to hurry up and come back again.

.

Cotton porn,
nigras making love to Jim Crows Thorns,
in world where to be black is scorned
where chasing freedom and turning the other cheek
for sake of family has mind,
skin and communities torn.
They got off on the travail,
though we prevail
beaten then put up for resale
at Mason Dixon's Retail;
but this won't be the stories you retell.

(Sing)

"Bring a wagon and all your pence,
new niggers have arrived.
Dress them good and proper
to catch a buyer's eye.
Break them in and teach 'em;
a good nigger abides
and if the wretch should run away,
beat them till they bleed,
then hang the niggers dry."
Don't let them get off on you.

BLACK GIRL MAGIC

Do you see the miracle that I conjure
and how it makes you weak in the knees?
Is it too obvious how my grace is escorted by the breeze?
Don't you see my brilliance and wish that you had it?
Aren't you mesmerized by the marvel of my black girl magic?
Don't you see the wonder and amazement
in my presence and my aura
or how I showcase the divinity
of being one with the Universe
and Mother Nature's daughter?

Don't you see the strength in my hair
kinky coily and poufy?
See as my crown wrestles gravity
and the wind simultaneously.
See the how it bounces back as a life lesson,
telling me, girl you better work it like you know it.
I know you can't help
but fall in love my black girl magic!

Don't you love it
when I twirl in all my splendour;
magic, beauty and elegance in a melanin blender.
Radiance of the sun gleaming,
the power of the universe beaming;
amazing, beautiful and classic
The ABC's of this masterpiece is a divine hat trick.
Won't you bask in the energy of my black girl magic?

My smile is black girl magic, my hair is black girl magic
My size is black girl magic, my strength is black girl magic.
It cannot be bottled, it cannot be sold,
it cannot depreciate, and it cannot be trolled.
It will not be reshaped, tossed aside or fixed,
it will not be gentrified or remixed, you better recognise
the dopeness of my black girl magic.

My peace, my happiness
is black girl magic
My joy and my success
black girl magic.
I'm dope and I'm blessed
elevating above the mess.
Welcome to the party of the authentic me
this black girl magic is here for eternity.

Genexodus II

With no mercy, the elements ruthlessly feast
upon the frailties of my timeworn bones;
truthfully, I suffer daily with many, yet I lie alone.
Failing to find peace as my oppressors sleep,
I am compelled to reminisce in the savagery
of this peerless cold, shivering—
with the tranquillity
of discomfort as my main console.
What's more, is for another night I'm reminded
of the peaceful comfort of our handmade homes,
all while turning in turmoil
inside this creature with great sails
that they have now chained us to in rows.

And these shackles

These shackles befriend me
as they grant warmth and comfort
convincing me that they,
unlike Judas, will never change;
I am perplexed as to how now,
I'm in the womb once more,
but of something completely strange.
I'm captive, held against my will, because
we've been betrayed by the ones of us
tormented by the worst of us.
My entire village, root of a nation,
the last of our people, parcelled off then mistreated,
badly bloodied by brutish beatings.
Each blow reminds us that though we are united,
we are still defeated...

LEGACY OF BITTERNESS

It was the best I could've done with what was given to me,
and I wasn't given much to begin with.
These were bad times for negroes across America.
We only had Jim Crow, his political cronies,
crooked cops and bloodthirsty racists. Times was so hard we had to
breathe in whispers when we spoke about freedom,
even if it was far from a possibility. I had a wife who died unfortunately,
so aside from my life, my son was the most important thing;
but how could I raise him? Each year raised meant he was closer
to being theirs to raze at the end of the day,
we were nigger farmers cultivating moving targets cased in melanin.
We planted what they consumed, the bright eyes of our legacy blinked
its first time and opened its pupils to doom.

We did our best, taught him to honour his word and always show respect,
but what if their predators felt equality was only realistic with ropes and chains
decorating our hands, feet and necks? Still we taught them our best:
a legacy of fear and self-denial. We taught them the truth we were denied,
we gave them whatever we had, lying to ourselves that we had something.
Fully aware, we passed down ideals and poverty, working to death,
simultaneously handing down debts, but we were free: free to be mistreated,
free to be ignored, free to burn, free to hang, free to never complain,
free to be hurt but never show pain. We were freer at birth,
seeing our children born and en route to the afterlife,
but truth is we were never free, and the chains that kept us together
tore us apart and that was our greatest legacy.
Darkness subjected isn't darkness removed. So we caved in our anger,
became bitter, and our children paid; we slaved and they got the exchange:
relations strained and family estranged. We did the best with what we had:
ignorance encased in misguided hope, we traded silence for our kids' life
because maybe they had the code in their DNA to cope.

We told them to respect family and friends because we never knew
when it would be time to pay respects to our families or friends.
The only surprises we had were birthdays and funeral arrangements.
We taught them their rules, aware it was broken; we conformed for sake of life,
swallowing dreams was easier than swallowing pride. Taking the pain,
and then being blamed for your lack of success: what were we supposed to do?
We crippled ourselves only to be walked over by you. We toiled, just so you could be
comfortable another day; we fought and scraped for you to have another plate.
We gave our bodies to death so you wouldn't feel any burden of ours or our parents'
weight. We gave you life and we may have given you a legacy of bitterness,
forget not that we too are familiar with the taste I guess one day you'll learn about
taking the crooked with the straights.

The Black Closet

Gee: Is anyone there? Can you hear me?
I'm scared to be an aberrance or an oddity.
I'm scared to look out because I've been shamed to look in.
I don't want to come out, but the more I remain
the more they complain about it.
I'm not being true to self, and family is refusing to help.
They don't want me, or my kind
they don't regard the crippling hypocrisy that's ferocious inside.
I hear them and their jokes:
the same words line up like prison bars and others like daggers
when I hear them and their quotes.
Too often I cry upon deaf ears, scared to be seen,
because it'll cause a scene and I don't want the attention;
I just want to be completely me,
not just parts yet to be assembled, or pieced away on layaway.
I want to express myself without the fear of ridicule,
without the fear of being judged,
or the fear of being made fun of.

I'm scared: is courage or freedom on sale at the supermarket?
Is it on sale online? Is self on a discount
that I may gather for my entire self?
I need to know so that I may take steps of boldness into my journey.
Instead, I dodge common tell-tale signs
to ward off those who suspect that I am suspect.
I act accordingly, deceiving others while I, programmed on auto-lie,
decompose as I continually compromise.
I became less invincible and tears became invisible as they fall from my eyes.
I subtract myself from myself, and left alone with all of me inside dying.
I hope for light, I hope for meaning, I hope for strength,
I hope to one day come outside
and that my life will be judged only on content of character,
not who or how I identify from the depths of my soul inside.
They hate me, but not more than the me they've forced me to be;
I hate me, as much as you hate what I hide,
I hate the me you see and smile with in ignorance
as I jester before your eyes: a clown, clad in a barrage of lies.
Can you hear me or my cries? Do you see me? Deep down inside?
Do you care if my truth offends?
Or do I for sake of your comfort have deathly déjà vus
as I die for you, while I die inside.

It's OK (Frustrated)

We became whatever was necessary to survive the times:
a punching bag, an emasculating guilt trip,
their wives most hated sex toy.
We transformed into whatever fed the children.
A circus act, we kept contorting,
broken while our husbands died for nonconforming,
We became nurse and counsellor at night-time,
consoling and calming my husband,
convincing myself while telling my babies:
it's okay, baby. I promise you it's gon' be okay.

We grew tired of seeing our men broken and beaten,
bloody floors and beds from whipped backs and open heads.
We took the pounding from massa
whether we didn't want to or had to.
So as our owner grabs my hand
and walks me to his empty bedroom,
I'm consoling and calming my husband
convincing myself while telling my baby:
It's okay, baby. I promise you it's gon' be okay.

We got tired of neglecting our children
while feeding theirs and while not feeding ours
they fed our children to gators,
the same material that made the shoes we had to clean.
Maybe that's why we shined them shoes
as though we was seeing our baby one last time.
My baby picking cotton, hoping everything's alright
'til he comes home and he's ready to die—
but if he leaves, who's gon suffer with me by my side?
So to survive, I tell my him: It's okay, baby!
I promise it's gon' be okay, just trust me, alright?

I'm only good if I make no mistakes
and that so happens to be this fateful day:
now massa mad and his missus adding fuel to the fire
calling me a an adulteress, a whore and a liar
telling him she always told him this was the case.
Now he twixt a rock and a hard place
and it ain't enough that he bloodied my face;
Massa gotta make a lesson outta me.
So while he walks me to my death,
the only thing I have left to do—
consoling and calming my husband,
convincing myself while telling my babies:
It's okay, baby. I promise you, you gon be okay.

Take Flight

You can be anything you want to be,
today you gon' see!
You can touch the sky,
all you need to do is believe.
Look up in the almighty skies
where you'll be immortalized,
bringing tears to your family's eyes.
You made it, like some before you;
blazing a flame for the future,
showing others what to do and not do.

Just look at you!
You made us so proud!
Listen as you scream aloud!
Look how angelic you look as you take off

from the ground.
It's time, little nigger,
it's time.
Take flight, little nigger,
take flight.
Rope around your neck,
little nigger,
is it tight?

Kick and scream, little nigger,
tonight's the night you die.
Take flight, little nigger,
take flight.
Is you dead, little nigger?
He good dead, all right.

GENEXODUS III

Grammah: do I still tell this story?

See, they bash us and they bash us
'til they begin to wheeze,
then they stop to breathe, one of few reprieves;
and there we dream about our children and our homes,
temporarily forgetting the coming maltreatment
'til the mastery of this foreign brutality is repeated.

And without fail...

We cringe as our mothers' mothers
weep to the soundtrack of their daughters' screams
accompanied by the sounds of our
ineffective chants of "peace! Peace, please"
failing to drown out these ungodly atrocities,
and we would complain,
but the more we complain,
their acts of indifference are raised.

And we ... are so razed
that we hide our pride for the sake of our lives,
telling ourselves whatever we need to,
only to be eaten by the turmoil that's also raping us inside.
This misery totally muzzles our speech,
and when we are silent, our silence is impossibly deep.

Picture standing on top of the highest mountain,
then keenly searching through the deepest seas,
listening for the sound of plankton sneeze.
(immensely impossible)

The Bag Lady

It is a skill to find comfort in the difficult places.

A step here, a step there, an adjustment here, another soon to come.
A bag here, a bag there, her task today is almost done.
Every day she picks up the burden of her ancestors,
the burden of her future and the burden within herself. Contempt mixed
with content: the legacy passed down to her with tears and regret.
She steps, burdened, with no place left to fit luggage: the first container
a bag of pain, a bag which strains and a bag of complaints. She pulls it everywhere
she goes, afraid of being too miserable, too nagging and afraid of being unwanted
or avoided. She carries it and screams all her worries in; all her doubts
and insecurities she shovels in. no one hears and no one knows the scars
from lessons she's learned before.

A step here then a step there with an adjustment soon to come;

a bag here, a bag there, her task today is almost done. Hopeful (deep sigh)
because of stories passed on about hardships of how her greats,
her grandparents feasted on failed gods as they laid down
on the feces infested hardships. She's come a long way as she presently
situates another bag for the future. A sly smile, a hidden dance,
when no one's around- bags get placed down as she sings and youthfully prances
around. The second container a bag of hope, a bag love and a bag of happiness
for days; she pulls and lugs it everywhere, when clouds reign on her sunny parade
or more so when her situations cannot be assuaged. She opens her joyful burden bag
that is made to alleviate what she alone cannot mitigate. Too cautious to scream
and be heard, for hope too often is more delicate than whispered words.
So she hopes in silence and wishes in secret
while picking up all she put down only to
make...
A step there then a step here with an adjustment soon to come;

a bag here, a bag there, her task today is almost done. She carries it all in this one,
the future she sees and the success she believes. For her family and
all their comfort, they only go forward as much as she does and it could end if they
don't take on the legacy of bearing up those before you. She brings death
with each step and life in another. She is the bag lady, burdened by the invisibility
of intuition, steps in discomfort so her children can walk in fruition.
She steps in pain, towards joy for a future she might not see. Worth the sacrifice
and sleepless nights, worth the disappointments,
silenced cries and watery eyes. Worth every step, worth every adjustment
just to continue accepting a progressive form
of settling for greener days in their children's pastures,
each step ensuring her befores don't affect their hereafters...
A step there then a step here with an adjustment soon to come;
a bag here, a bag there, another mothers sacrifice of a life, almost done.

...steps...

The Hot Potato

Sings*
*Pass it, pass it. don't let it burn you
Pass it to anyone when it's your turn to.
Hot potato in the air, burning where it lands
Pass it to your loved ones, burning in their hands.
Hot potato, hot potato, one-two-three
Pass it to another nigger that looks like me.*

We threw it in innocence, unaware of the dangers therein;
so day after day we played, figuring out new ways to win.
We created elaborate moves, burgeoning cool,
see hot potato was merely a tool used to pass the time.
All the while we played, we never knew
that it was rewiring our subconscious hard drive.
We just sang the songs our elders taught us
without the story behind the scenes;
we were taught to aim for Malcolm's success by Martin's means.
We didn't know the impact or the parallels being drawn.
We just played, getting caught red-handed
in a losing game as time had gone on.

Hot potato wasn't just a game, it was cognitive dissonance;
pitching amongst ourselves Lynchstory,
Samboology and Uncle Tomism
with extra lessons in Crab Theory,
We hung from the kicked buckets we made it out of.
How were we supposed to know
we tossed a legacy of slavery and fear?
Present met the past with the ties that bind
as we undertook understudies in archaeological remixes,
noose-held effigies fought gravity and rebellion in
Mason Dixon's avant-garde fashion show titled:
A Southern Nigger's Runway in the Sky.
We saw the signs, but normalcy made us compliant;
the in-cult catered to a wide audience they inculcated.
To survive, we accommodated their lies;
hot potato compromised our lives,
hot potato reheated the scars in our mind.

Truth is, we were passing the blame, photoshopping the pain
constantly passing the buck mesmerized by the hoax
that there was a winner in the game.
We ought to have been ashamed, but we were kids who identified
the Coonmanship of Niggernometry by a different name.
Our fathers and forefathers tried to protect us
and while they learned, so they died,
martyring in vain for our future to no longer be the same...

and unaware, we sang their disdain,
intertwining codes and signs for help and change,
they toiled for a legacy and we wane
faster than the fruits of their posterity...
Unsung heroes whose stories fade away from our memory;
so we just kept passing the innocence parceled in ignorance.
You know, playing the game, making do, with tampered scales
brushing off that the maintenance of bondage lacked no upgrade.
Caucus trickery with sleight of/and underhanded pitching
ensured the hurt and the damage went unrealized:
"missing the large picture metaphors and puns
we just kept reenacting the pain, the picture master fully sketched,
and we were always painted criminals in the frame."

When we were hurt, we threw.
Hopeless, we threw. Killed, we threw, blatant injustices we threw,
culture appropriation we threw. Rewriting history, we threw.
Truth is, we threw away the hurt
because it was something we couldn't handle,
something we couldn't deal with. Something we never knew
even though it crippled our minds and took our lives.
There were those of us who were strong enough to bear the heat,
but once the pressure was on, you were out the game.
They left with no legacy or memory, their fingerprints on the potato
remolded and reheated to prevent another bold soul.

We passed that potato into glory.
Subconsciously betraying ourselves because of the HISstory
of how we barbarian neanderthals evolved from caged and zooed livestock.
We passed it, singing soul-stirring negro spirituals,
showing off how well we dealt with the ignorance of our oppression,
while our oppressors unfazed by the skill of our upkeep
as long as we passed the heat, we'd never be out the kitchen.
Niggers being cooked in the pot of racism and inequality;
hot potato, hot potato, sears lynchism down to the core.
hot potato, hot potato, respawns niggers more and more.
This hot potato that holds our freedom, our boldness
our future, our voice and our potential, in the air soars
How long will we play? 'Til there's no one left?
Or 'til the potato is mashed on the floor?

Sings
*Pass it, pass it, don't let it burn you
Pass it to anyone when it's your turn to
Hot potato in the air, burning where it lands
Pass it to your loved ones, burning in their hands.
Hot potato, hot potato, one-two-three
Pass it to another nigger that looks like me.*
*

Please don't!

Illuminati Love Affair IV: Juss Stockholm

captive and lover - infatuated and enamoured
captor and warden - thoroughly bitter and unsatisfied;
what manner of love is this
chasing after the crumbs of a one sided relationship.
The unacceptable mortal
salivating after these diseased morsels.
What a shame, the desire of the slave
to be wholly submissive while they remain in disgrace.
The unfair exchange...a body of lies and wicked surprise
discomfort deconstructed hope into demise,
revelation unfolding before their very eyes,
turning the other cheek being meek,
begging permission to be and to speak,
what a sight as captive gift their lives to them which lie...

A shame to see- ashamed as he
is here again, left desolate- void of might.
Struggling inside for reason or rhyme
whisperingly nervous he questions why,
but is dismissed and told it'll better next time.

He becomes still, disquieted within
looking for proof of truth
though it comes packaged in beguile's disguise.
Distraction doled out 'til it tranquillised and just then disaster strikes.
Disappointed, he breaks down and cries
protesting the pain of the truth he is so willing to deny.
Hoping still, subconsciously against his will.
Begs, on knees with hands gesticulating his crying pleas
to the woman he thinks is the one
that will finally give him piece of the peace
that will make him whole and free

He begs, and pleads for her to fulfil his needs,
'til she spurns his attempts.
Filled with resentment she deems him unworthy,
he laments the affairs of the heart
amidst the injustices and disregard.
He still pines- to his captor, his lover, - this actor
whom he convinced is the one to believe- in us.
So he forgives, with misplaced trust
ignoring the facts, the deadly stats
believing the scripture upon which he was fostered
favourite book: Acts of the Impostor.

He won't choose to learn
thinking Love covers a multitude of sins,
it does cover the world except those that look like him.

.

But one good turn, rivals its failures and she just unpacks her nature.
Refusing to give him his day to be right
aware of his efforts, aware of his plight,
recalcitrant to his cause, dismissive of his fight.
All because he can never be whole
or white enough to matter on her scale.
So time and time again,
she redefines the parameters for equality
in the overall scheme of things
until he's right in the cross fire
and on the wrong end in scheme of things.
Here we go again one more try;
still and again- white ears never heard melanin cries.

To him, Joss just lies!
She who sees all but to him remains blind.
This fool- head over heels in love
with all she stands for after all she's done
This dominatrix - makes right what men make ill.
She fakes sick, then everyone conforms to her will
while she mindlessly bends to her pimping grandfathers' whim.
Masked and hooded with sinister grins
all Miss represents- is a facade that misrepresents.
And still obeisant to her transient demands and wants
his captivity she flaunts - doggishly he keeps coming back
Pavlov's dog in melanin form.
Justice never gave a fair shot at equality or unity
and until she does- in this quandary he shall remain
slave to her ways,
yet still seeking a change of everything that she displays.

The image of truth she betrays- punished he became
as though love was synonymous with pain and trials
sipping hope from poisoned vials.
Thinking we were never enough
heartbroken we drank from envenomed flasks,
spiked with more malcontent
than the bitterness of the inhabitants that jumped ship
from the first continent...
and if he ever tried to be free- it'd only be with death and misery
so his only hope is to love- incommodiously
and inconveniently- tasting freedom and equality
with dirty spoons of invisibility.
Anxious for the moment Joss will do right,
only to be told- maybe next time.
And like moths to a light, or the naive to a lie.
He clings to the joss' tease,
sacrificing generations with genetic conformities,
singing "please, please! Do right by me or give me a sign
that you'll do right if not by me then for my children next time.

The fathers of joss just smiles, knowing that his prisoner
is too strung out to realise, too infatuated with being seen with equal eyes:
tells joss to hug them and give them a prize
a consolation and to remind them that they'll do better...
the next time... unawares that there has to be injustice
for them to even have a reason
to plead for better treatment the next time.
So he goes back to sleep and dreams of peace
and equality in the loving arms of the woman
who sees him as beneath and his presence a disease
but loyal to her duty she breathes a sigh of relief,
takes off the blind fold and removes the scales
kisses the lips of the face she calls Love by name.
Secretly they make love repeatedly, she convinces him needlessly
since he believes. Finally falling asleep
unawares of her willingness in the crime...
he closes his eyes, she puts on her blinds
kisses him on the forehead and smiles...
we'll see next time.

Genexodus IV

Grammah: crying
Our pain is that great, intensified by that deep,
and that's not even where our pain peaks!
Death is our worst fear and the only sense of freedom we see.

We have constantly relived this agony,
for seventy-eight moons
we have been dying off to the same routine
and there's been no change:
our daughters raped and our men slain.

Our legacy drowns and our strength wanes
yet still we row—and when we row,
we row to change in chains, in chains we've changed
to colossal cowards too afraid to be brave.

And as our history pales in a lifeless trail
of floating bodies that show you our voyage into hell,
we've become mere bread crumbs, tossed into oblivion
with less worth than those flung by Hansel and Gretel.

Truth is, we've come a long way,
from the overthrown bodies that have paved the road
for those cursed with the beautiful skin
of queens and kings.

Our deepest fear
is that we will be blamed for all your future mistakes
and if that be the case, then from all of us
who fought to be free with all of our might
only to be mutilated, buried overboard
violated and sodomized:
we apologize completely
for what you've ultimately become...

Black Phoenix

in tears
When the road being paved
has lost its most valued workers
and it seems as though
there will be no longer be a better way.
I will rise!

When our history has been pushed aside
in the face of our unjust demise,
from those with prejudicial eyes...
though it may be hard
I ... will rise

Rise above the defeat, rise above the hurt
rise even when my brothers
have been riddled with gunshots
and we have no answers why...
though I may be next,
I too will rise...

With heads held high
as fear evaporates in the sky
I am my brother's keeper
and sometimes the shoulders
for those who are
our most tearful weepers.
Though broken I may be
my strength prevents
my wailing cry, I will stand up
for if no one will...
I must ... I will rise

Though I may be days late
when I heard of your ill state
I was saddened and heartbroken
even now I shed tears
for one I've never met
never seen or made laugh.
For now my hopes of a future seeing you
will only be memories of dreams
that never came to pass.

For all that you have done
I am grateful for the impact
you made with your time;
and as you are, as I will be
a black phoenix for no matter the fire
I too will rise.

Black Closet II

Cys: Ayo wassup, king! Its crazy out there, ain't it?
I mean how do they expect us to live,
this can't go on for long. How long have you been in here?

Gee: Ever since I could remember, it's always been crazy.
But we're so divided on what we want and how we want it.

Cys: What you mean brehv?

Gee: I'm just saying we want things independently,
individually, not as a whole, not as a people.
We don't agree for progress; we only agree for points made.

Cys: Yeah, I see that, some side with law enforcement
more than the victim even before the whole story is out!
Can you believe that?! It's crazy!

Gee: C'mon, man, the full story only comes out
months after the verdict of "not guilty."

Cys: That's a stone-cold fact though!

Gee: Yeah, man, it's crazy out there;
it's like everybody is against us, even us!

Cys: I'm kinda glad it's people like you in our safe haven
that care about us and what we need as a people.
You should be out there with the others, man.
You got a lot of strong points, king!

Gee: Nah, I'm cool where I'm at;
it's crazy out there like you said.
They're killing good people and innocent people-
people with records and people without records,
people who comply and people who don't!

Cys: I don't understand, king. All that shit you just said
about doing stuff for us was fake? Just words?

Gee: Not at all. I mean them, but in this closet
is where I'm the safest
and sadly where I'm most prone to violence. Right here with us.

Cys: I don't understand, king! What's the point of you saying
we need us uniting for the sake of the progress of our people
if we don't put our ego to the side and do what we need to?

Gee: You tell me; we go in the closet to be safe and feel safe,
but I can't ever feel safe or be taken seriously
because of who I choose to love and how I choose
to sexually manifest my love?

Cys: Oh shit! You gay! Nah, you gotta go!
Look yo we don't need your kind in here, yo!
You setting our people back and preventing us from uniting.
Your people part of the emasculation of black men.
I thought you was a king! Ole queer quean ass nigga,
get outta here before I beat yo' bitch ass, lil' nigga!

Gee: Where tf am I spose to go now?

Cys: That really ain't my problem!
Get your bitch ass outta here
before you end up on the news like all the others!

CCXCIIXXXVII

"Son, that bitch a hoe!
All these black bitches be 'bout is twerking,
going on trips, leaving their bad ass kids
with their more ratchet but retired ass grandmothers
while they use EBT and WIC to buy alcohol fake hair.
Let's not even mention how they be tricking the system wit all that welfare.
They lazy, bruh! I can't stand them they so stuck up and bougie
and swear they all that. As a man I can't give 'em no respect
cuz they don't deserve it; they want everything given to 'em!
On my mama, these black bitches be doing the most.
But these latinas and white women, my nigga: they winning!
That's the wave, yo; they talk to you, they respect men and shit.
Yo, like, for real. Why black women can't be more like them?
These hoes ain't even real bro: fake lashes,
eyebrows, nails–fake e'erything;
all they want is another man's money.
Black bitches ain't shit, son.
Fuck 'em for real man, I'm done wid 'em. "
(deep sigh)
Truth is, sometimes we forget the medium
we took to get to where we are.
Whether a road, a boat or in some cases a birth canal.

Black women were used vehicles
that their black husband leased
and whenever that nigger gave trouble,
she went back to the dealer so he could be aligned.
This was the method on which they relied,
where behavior was revised and then modified.
Black woman, the symbol of strength, power and resilience
was repeatedly transformed into a cumpiece of disregard;
her husband's world ripped apart, along with her insides.
Zipped up pants accompanied with sinister laughs and spiteful smiles;
black women, served up and tossed to the side.
He cries and she only finds the voice to whimper and apologise.
That bitch? Tell me, is it our black woman you call that bitch?

Black woman, the greatest burden bearer of all time
had civilizations brought forth from her womb
only to spend a lifetime carrying nations
that never regarded her or her whip-scarred back!
You talking about that bitch? Lemme know...
Black women have been the standard for beauty and strength,
the symbol of resilience, love and sacrifice
yet they've been ridiculed and pushed to the side;
downplayed and mocked worst by those she needed
and whose life greatly benefitted from her perseverance.

You talking bout that bitch?

That bitch who knows your struggle?
That bitch who knows every strain of your pain?
Knows every millimeter of your potential?
She, who has the keys, the codes and the power
to enable more than anyone else could?

That bitch?

Listen, stars were never meant for human touch
'til slave masters convinced black men that the star of our melanin
wasn't as bright as his wife.
Fever della Jungle was a sought-after disease
whose cure was used to demean the color of the only woman
who could console, multiply
and bring joy better than anyone else could...
Black women, have been played and plagued
by rapists, murderers and scoundrels.
Black women, have been passed on but passed around
over and over again like stories around campfires,
discarded like marshmallow sticks
after they've been s'mored,
toaster strudelled and hostessed against their will!
You talking bout the Black Woman
who's been regarded as lower than a whore
and then left for the man
who loved her despite her many invasions?
Please tell me you aint referring to her as that bitch!
You talking about the Black Woman
who gave her lasts for you to have firsts,
who gave her milk without consent
to grow massa's babies stronger than her own
and raised her sons to be cooperative
so as to not have them die as her husband did?
Please tell me you aint referring
to the Black Woman as any kind of bitch!

She saw men who'd die for her do just that
as they took her lover, tarred him
and attached limbs to dismember him
and she raised sons as cowards so as to
have you not be re (dis)membered like him.
That bitch who gave her all with hope and love,
covering your unlimited flaws
with no return on her investments,
used 'til she was out of tune and no longer a muse,
the wear and tear of slavery,
an over-sexualized, cotton-picking instrument
is that bitch you bash and denigrate,
that bitch your words attempt to break down and destroy?

Listen to your insecurities perpetrating and perpetuating
an image that we can change
but instead we complain and continue to train the future generation
that they should be treated the same.
That bitch is not her name, that bitch is not her destiny,
that bitch is not her job.
The Black Woman is not a bitch, they are
our mothers, our sisters, our daughters, our lovers...
So please, blind, ignorant and hurt black man
please, for the sake of your fragile masculinity, stop projecting.

Genexodus V

To the men,
we apologize that you morphed from royalty
into gun-toting career prisoners
who desperately value the mating ritual
but abandon the priceless trophy that is your son.

To our daughters, we apologize
that the reality of us being molested
wasn't enough for you;
we are sorry that what our oppressors
were attracted to your sleazy parade for views.

We apologize for your godlessness,
for your poverty and hopelessness.

We apologize
one hundred times one hundred times
that we never came back
and left you all alone.
We apologize for the stereotypes,
for the unemployment and your broken homes;
we apologize that you use our sufferings as phantom pains;
the phantom pains of mental slaves
that serve as invisible ropes and chains
that hang and constrict
the unbridled power you let die within.

It's apparent you'd choose to suffer with us
rather than be successful in spite of us.
We had hoped your future wouldn't be as dim
as our blood-smeared skin.
We are truly sorry
that all of you walk around freely
in a world you were born in
only to be enslaved
in more ways than we've ever been.

The Audacity

I had the nerve...
to have a dream, a dream that hankered on the profound words of black kings,
who at the peaks of their lives met their demise by self-hating uncle toms
and willie lynch assassins. I believed an illusion so unreal, yet so pristine
that it hung ... HOPE higher than the beaten bodies of battered blacks
whose broken necks made sweet love to racist ropes.

East to west, lifeless bodies mocked the pendulum swing; the times changed,
but the positions didn't. Every generation of every nation faced relentless injustice,
due to the strength of the melanin in my skin. What could I have done
to deserve these impromptu death penalties, where breathing transforms
my livelihood into another unpunished casualty? What place is safe for me
while I sit in silence, praying to God for him to tell my persecutors
to "Stop The Violence"!

I've been profiled and denied basic rights. I've been accused and abused,
been tased and pepper sprayed, illegally placed under arrest, and even choked to
death. I've been mistreated without cause repeatedly; I thought I was human,
'til I found out bullets were the only vitamins that cured my caucasian deficiency.
As my beautiful black skin was the green light for red neck vigilantes
and white cops in blue to take every liberty in taking my life and liberties,
all while hiding their true colors behind doctoral degrees,
police badges and white sheets.

The stench of racism lingers still, and the likelihood of justice and equality
is just as bright as the "darkness" of my skin and no matter the progress,
our road to freedom is just as clear as the beaten face of Emmitt Till.
Imagine, I'm supposed to dare to dream but they don't tell you it's dear to dream.
When our oppressors dress us in high fashion shackles
whitewashing our history, then stealing our identity,
successfully convincing the blind and the sleep
that there is nothing we need, and we should be happy at least we're free.

How many times must we see with our own eyes our brothers and sisters die?
Conscious or sleep, blacks on both sides meeting the same demise
and recrying the same cries; marching and protesting
with reused picket signs, while our murderers hide under the guise
of being traumatized for fear of being victimized. Yet you have the audacity
to tell me I'm free when you call us creatures, then steal our features,
castrate our leaders and silence our teachers.

I'm sorry, but I can no longer pretend
like I don't worry if the next death is mine.
I'm scared ... wondering if
leaving my house signals the last time
my loved ones will see my smile.

Lord knows I've tried to be polite,
playing the part that massa likes,
but my back aches and I'm losing my mind
slaving while perfecting the shuck and jive.
It's time to take a stance for the chance to be free.
They kill us and we kill us, but we are not our enemies.
We are far from the niggers, niggas and bitches they paint us to be;
we are royalty, kings and queens!
Let's wake up then stand up to unite, and fight for what we need
because, my people, we are dying,
peacefully chasing after a dream
that can only be taken by violent means.

BELIEVE IT LOUD:

I AM BLACK AND I AM PROUD.

WELCOME TO
GRAMMERLIN SQUARE

HOME OF
THE GRANDMENTALSTATION

ALL ABOARD
THE GRANDSCENDENCE

NEXT STOP:

DERELICTS ROAD

DIVINE

Vagrant Alley

THE SOUL OF A MAN

It is captive to the sound of the voices and their irrepressive goading, t
heir tone prophetic and foreboding. Repetitiously being coaxed and cajoled,
this independent being clearly remote-controlled. In essence, a piece of a whole on
hold, oblivious to its willful participation, your everyday Truman Show.
These sounds move my being, eerily as though 'twere a divine flute;
whichever tune, it soothes and the mouse trapped will follow suit.
The sound is eclectic and alluring, but it is also silent.
Nature's snake charming melodies moves my entirety
against its will with much ease. Each note that crescendos brings me
to my knees as I weep at the state of my affairs, beseeching
any deity to have mercy, with doubt filling every aspect of my pleas(e).

The soul of a man is a bedouin, travelling as much as he travails
in a land of unknowns, wrapped up in like ilk, tiled by
the uncontrollable disasters which bullies it to realize
its ever-fleeting mortality. It beckons to the afterlife,
especially if there is another, after life.
It just bides its time, while being paid no mind, until its host is damaged
and reflecting on regrets or is pressed for time at the tail end of their life.
How do you grasp the unseeable that is also unfathomable?
What is the value of the invisible and the untouchable?
What is its worth, and from whence does its importance come?
Have you any answers hid, or are you likewise oblivious?
Because the soul of a man is silent and intangible, unseen and untouched,
simply unaccounted for: a last minute plaything and the unplayable toy.

It rots away into oblivion while its host despairs,
unaware of the perpetuity into which it steers/stares.
The stepchild of our being is nescient of his being and potency
as it writhes away in utter redundancy and though it writhes,
it's canvassed in silence, with neither heart nor mind privy to its cries.
It occasionally peeks when both are damaged and faced
with what beyond eternity lies. This soul of this man seeks
refuge throughout the daunting impossibilities of attaining
any semblance of sanity. What's worst is much less success
is granted in the spontaneous anarchy with which it's rapt;
and that which it's wrapped in, it is indubitably trapped in.

The soul (if one calls it that) of a man is afflicted as he hears
what his host isn't privy to, simultaneously incapable of fighting
the illegal downloads of all things spiritual. An incapable guardian angel
who receives all the weight of the broken scales from the heart and mind's display,
it registers all the pain and burdens and affords nothing even on divine layaway.
This soul, weary from repeated mistakes on every plane,
is burdened with what happens after it's all said and done, because maybe,
even after all is done, it might just have begun.

This soul...

The Vagrant

down the street where it smells and no one goes
lives a dirty mind; from when, no one knows.
he walks and talks all by himself
till he passes out to take his rest.
we stop and listen from time to time
to hear the belligerence spewing from his mind.
he's right, he's wrong and all over the place
but he asks us questions satiating our curious taste

he's dirty and smelly, mom says we should feed him,
it is our christian chore,
father says don't feed the strays
him speaking is no different than a zoo lion's roar.
he talks about us,
and how we treat each other
like a bother and it's reflected with him.
we respond to one another based on the anguish within.
I like him; he makes funny faces and says we are the future,
and that time, truth and love are the only instruments
that remove life's sutures.
he says "life's a tutor, life's a suitor, while it never suits ya"!

I like him a lot; mom calls him tolerably dirty,
Father says he's a spy or an international agent!
But he calls everyone a friend
while he's known as The Vagrant.

Worlds Before

Coins, anyone? Change, anyone?
Spare some change? Anything helps
I could use some pennies for your thoughts? Anyone here?
A few minutes of conversation, anyone care?
Oh, bless you. Bless your heart,
kind lady! Thank you!

May I ask...
what if we've all been here before,
and we here now are all the remnants of the damnation
worlds past- given another chance with another
different set of circumstances to see
if we would be a better version of our unknown selves?
What if déjà vu is real and parallel universes
are our past selves converging a point where habits our thoughts align?
What if the new you is aware of the current
you, but the current you puts the déjà vu to a past you?

Do you think we've been here before?
What about angels? Do you think about them?
Do we know from whence they came?
Or how they really got their name?
What if God made worlds
before the world we now know
and each world faced their respective judgement;
what if we had foreworldfathers before our forefathers?
What if the angels we hear of in the bible
were goodly humans who lived extraordinary lives
and were chosen to live forever based on their good deeds?

What if they only helped their descendants
but this world was made without that awareness of the line
so angels help no one?
What if there's an angel union and Christ was the Jimmy Hoffa
because their ancestors kept using them
all the time and they couldn't be everywhere
like their creator so they complained
and because they were the saints of their time and were saved,
God said okay and allowed a mediator,
but they had to wait for a new world for it to come into play?

Change, anyone? Could you spare a nickel?
A dime? Maybe just your time?
Anyone, you there? Penny for a thought?

SINOLUTION

Change, anyone? Anyone have any change?
Change for the world, change for the homeless?
Change for a vagrant? Change for me?
Penny for a thought. Conversation, anybody?
Thank you, little one, thank you!

They say earth and everything in it was made by a supreme being
whose contingency rests upon and within himself.
They said he said it was perfect because he made it and because he's
perfect and perfection comes from him.
They say he makes no mistakes. They said he created (days one, two, three,
four, five, six). But did you know that each thing he created set the foundation
for the thing he created after it? The first needs only him, the second needs the first,
and the third needs the second? Fourth, the third ... all the way 'til the sixth
needing the fifth. It all goes back to him who made perfection, back
to the uncaused cause who first caused everything.
He made everything perfect.

This is what the good book says, no? After he made all things, he said it was good.
Good as in perfect. He was satisfied, as it pleased him. The creator was satisfied with
his creation. It was perfect, and it was stabilized and maintained solely by him.
Creation, maintained by perfection, deems change unnecessary, no?
What tweaks are required for perfection to continue its execution?
What upgrades, what reconstructions, are required? Pray tell.
Is perfection, the state where failure does not exist,
when since has perfection needed to evolve, and how?
If the creation lacks nothing,
what need of change at any point is necessary?

Penny to continue the thought?
More for a finished one? Thank you!

What need have we to maintain perfection if the contingencies that be,
are all tied to a perfect being whose sustenance is found within himself?
If he fails, all fails, if he doesn't continue, his dependents fail,
same goes if he chooses. Isn't our (human) choice by virtue of his ultimate decision
moot? Take a second. All things created were made perfect by the design
of a being who is, in the most potent and purest sense, faultless and infallible.
What goes wrong with perfection? All I'm saying is in the beginning
was perfection, and flaw knew no life and had no existence.
A question I have is, what day was sin created on and which
day is it contingent upon? Because sin came, and when it did,
it disrupted perfection. It disrupted and jolted the harmony that was
established; flaws came to be, fault found life,
came crying as all newborns do when they're brought to the light
for the first time and there at the entrance of sin
was the principle of evolution born.

Evolution is defined as change over time, but for something to evolve
there had to have been a standard to evolve from. The beginning is as simple
as can be, then foiled by sin, and from there came such complexities as survival
of the fittest which leads to other complexities such as the elimination
or extinction of species and the remodeling of the food chain

Did the forecreatures prey,
were there such things as predators let alone those of the apex kind?

Evolution requires a standard by which one can compare what was evolved
from and what it was evolved to, we can't begin at evolution.
As evolution became more pronounced and more established, we've lost animals,
types of humans, each type of each era the pinnacle of that age and all
incapable of being successful or efficient as the time before.
Animals were retiring way before sports athletes were, think about it!
The earth was changing and forcing its inhabitants to adapt or die,
at no point caring about the losses it accrued. For while the earth
made its changes, it got rid of once upon time essentials that were now phased
out and no longer necessary. Imagine a ship whose integrity
has been compromised; doesn't one, in essence,
throw away items that, though they may have been of importance,
are now only dead weight or pointless going forward, no? Luxury items
that don't fit the requirements for the journey ahead are discarded.
Isn't that what nature does and has done: kept those, as she continues
into her deteriorating slumber?

"Get outta here vagabond, you've been here too long, it's time to go"

Change, anyone? For the world?
For earth?
For me? Anyone?
Please? (ship compromised)

One Crown, One Sovereign Lord I

My Master and my King, eternal Sovereign and ruler of all,
holiness exists because You do and righteousness finds its origin in You.
Awesome immaculacy, splendor above all wonders,
hallowed is Your Word, even more sacred is Your name.
You are worth above worth,
the orchestrator and maintainer of all, without exclusion.
I beseech you, Holy LORD,
purge me thoroughly with the omnipotence of Your holiness.
I beg of thee, LORD, that the fire in your eyes sears my every transgression,
as you know my depraved heart and my filthy mind.
I am a wasteland of insignificance, spiritually barren and destitute.
Awaken me, my spirit's Master;
quicken me with your life sustaining HOLY Paraclete.
Puppeteer my obedience
through the frustrating tribulations that ceaselessly come.
Commandeer my soul and force my surrender,
invade my heart and mind;
no strength have I, 'cept that which You've parceled;
no merit can I attain 'cept Christ impute;
no will have I 'cept that which is lent by You.
Devour my habits and wake me new in You;
I am unworthy, a view detestable before holiness.
Overwhelm my mouth, that my speech may speak of Thee;
uproot the spring of bitter reaction in me
that I may be a single lane of praise and thanksgiving.
I tread a path of waywardness, rushing into pleasure.
My mind tirelessly tiles a path my sinfulness has mapped out.
I am relentless in my wickedness,
in pursuit of all things pleasurably evil,
armed with swift feet and a quicker mouth,
ready to go and say whatever will gratify
my unappeasable greediness.
LORD, save me;
heal my scores of infirmities;
carry them on a never-ending journey
to find weakness in Your most perfect strength.
I am desperate for a manifestation
of Your divine work to move in me,
bring life to this helpless dead,
forgive and restrain my reckless evil,
for it seemeth right to do ...
I am yours, save me...

Doubt Chronicles Part I

It's been a while since I've been here before you; and it feels like lifetimes
since I've knelt or surrendered. Seems like no matter how much I know,
my habits flow hand-in-hand in forgetting your supremacy.
I've gone on too long thinking I'm capable, or being humbled.
Life has been hard lately; I think that was the alarm that prompted my return.
You're my gas station and my fuel when I leave until the world depletes me,
but I always- even though I know better, I always come back on E.
I hate that our relationship revolves around what I need,
but that's how they taught me–that you'll supply all my needs.
I don't even know if this is how I'm supposed to call unto you.
The bible is in old English; I don't know if I should mix it up
with how I learned and how the bible uses English.
I'm conflicted, I want to pour my heart out, but the atheists
say you aren't real, and some of my close friends don't believe in you.
Then, my Christian friends believe in different versions of you,
different ways to get to you, and I have a few Muslim friends who
say something else completely different. I think it's best if I just come
to you in my own way and say what's on my heart and what's on my soul.
I mean, if you are God, it's not like you haven't seen it or aren't aware.
Maybe my perspective is something that you can't see that well,
kinda like how I can't see yours as well. Now that I think about it,
maybe this was the plan all along, and all you need for me to do
is come to terms with what you made me out to be in the first place.
I don't know, but it shouldn't be this hard...

a conflicted vagabond...

Outcomes Part I

We love us a good result.
We relish an outcome that we can not only share with our loved ones,
but also hope to tell our grandchildren just how awesome we were.
We like to look good; we love even more to be impressive.
We love when a good plan—our ideas, dreams and goals—comes through.
But... when the outcome doesn't suit us,
is that when we worry most? Feel most let down? Downcast?
How do you feel when your super powers are helpless,
especially when you want to be most helpful?
What's the outcome when what you want isn't possible,
isn't happening nor is it close to anything that you'd like?

What's the outcome?

When you don't know how to move and you're afraid of what next will happen,
what's the outcome? Do we not, run swiftly to God in hopes of persuading
the subservient Holy Genie that the outcome suits us both,
so we pray with words that would sound like it's what WE want?
Aren't our cries, better yet gripes, prayers and desires, puppeteered by our greed?
Do they not find their foundation in pride whose streams
flow steadily into the sea of selfishness; is it not true that our eyes
see "I" and because we are also (selfish); therefore,
we see enviously and nearsightedly?

Do we not heap up prayers and decrees that only, in turn, seek to increase
our independence and subtract our need for the illimitable transcendence?
We are so self-driven we often seem to be missing the large picture,
solely focused with ideals that pass away and compound the issue we initially sought
to be free from. (Parallel* Cue one of the many commercials that attempts to fix one
thing, but the side effects are worse than the sickness that afflicts us.)

Truth is, we are rife with issues, deficiencies, vulnerabilities and insecurities;
replete with pain, disappointments and regrets. All we continually seek are flashy
bandages that hide the discolouring of our wounds and the sounds of our pain.
We constantly apply our best makeup in the rain, our life,
a cyclical evolution of angst that we pretend to manage, when truth is,
our baggage got so heavy we started accommodating and adapting to it.
Burden bags we once dragged on the floor of our lives now come
with wheels and trolleys that we push around,
and unfairly unpack on anyone we love ...

The Bottom Rung

Man, regardless of how great he is or becomes, no matter how ground breaking, in spite of his intelligence, influence or affluence–man is and always has been at the bottom rung of the proverbial totem pole. No matter how evolved he becomes or how aware he ends up, he's still truly and essentially will be the bottom rung. This is not to disregard the comeuppance of the exquisite or extraordinary feats he's accomplished over many a millennia; this isn't to throw mud or shade on his innumerable achievements. This is merely a matter of truth, notwithstanding how skewed you believe my conclusion to be. I'm not asking you to believe, but if you feel compelled to, do as you feel, and if you feel compelled to dismiss it, do so freely.

Man is unmitigatedly dependent, and almost everything he depends on, depends on something else to survive. In essence, man is perennially on life support; he is hooked up to series of contingencies for total sustenance. What sustains him needs to be sustained, and what sustains his sustainer needs to be maintained. Man, according to the biblical narrative (which some take offense to because of the God and his deeds or misdeeds, depending on context and, of course, who you asked) was made last. For clarity's sake, Man was created last. Which logically could mean he came into an existence that didn't need him, nor did it require his existence or his input. The air and the galaxy didn't ask him to be curious; they didn't ask him to count or explore. The seas never told him to dive in to be curious and investigate; the animals never asked him to be fed. Everything he came and saw existed before him and settled in before him.

Therefore, man is a disruption, the oversized insect and virulent pest that caused the aberrances we now suffer from. The cause of the problem is man, the procurer of the problem is man, and man without knowledge of initial purpose has been on a warpath to correct an issue that he knows not how to correct or what he needs to do in order to do so. Man is at fault for his misery, the janitor for his suffering and despite all the learning, he is still the unlearned, scientist in his adversity; all his endeavors propagate his suffering; his evolution propels it, and his ego makes it unmissable. The divine marksman of abject failure, the ultimate parasite that migrates simultaneously giving nature apocalyptic migraines, man–the absent-minded and indebted zookeeper, forgot his purpose and interferes with everyone else's.
- the Vagabond -

Ruin Me

"In dire need of You greatly,
in need of Your love, grace and mercy;
I am Yours. Save me."
-the Vagabond
Ungratefulness flirts with me constantly these days; repeatedly,
I anchor my strength firmly in my confidence, and all the results
proceed conclusively in failure. I wade, hopeless and dejected,
in the guilt of missing the mark yet again, hiding under the radar until
the gripping shadow of remorse and self-reproach subsides; and as soon as it does,
I am ready to strengthen my desire, better my results, only to fail again and feel,
once more, responsible. My weaknesses are spread about, surrounding me a
s enemies' border outnumbered foes; in their solidarity, they blatantly taunt
my frailties, all the while goading me to desperately exert my false
sense of strengths and skewed views of excellence.

My ego twists my arms and impels me to test their matchless record, convincing me
every time that my next attempt will be the best one yet. Over and over again,
they have proven cunning, and my attempts are still ... futile. I've come
to realise my weakness is a disadvantage, and my confidence
in my strength and trust in my own abilities is compounding my flimsiness
and worsening a visible limitation... Pride has been, and still is,
my adamantium-free Achilles' heel, for whenever I take stock in
my capabilities and in my wherewithal, failure grossly
and most noticeably abounds. My weakness persistently fails me, and yet,
still, with much tenacity, I feel it necessary to prove it otherwise
with my strength, my knowledge and my understanding–
a most incapacitating trifecta.

My knowledge is limited, and my understanding can walk no more than
a newborn baby; ultimately, whatever I ascribed and concluded as strength
perpetually fails me. What sense of hopelessness have I subjected myself to–
what inheritance have I been so quick to grasp in feeble hands too small
to hold such great a thing as hope? Alas, I am convinced that the root of
my confidence is innate and is indubitably crippling. I hope that You (El Olam)
render me weak, with You as the only source of strength. May you, while
You give me my daily bread, suffer me to admit, both consciously
and subconsciously, that You alone are my constant supplier of strength.
Remove from me confidence and subtle self-elevators which propel me
to desolation and lowly places whose foundation is pride.
Ruin me continually for the beauty of Your majesty.

I am yours, save me.

Teach Me Your Ways (A song)

teach me your ways,
that I may worship you
keep me on the narrow side
with the righteous few.
hold me to your bosom, lord;
keep me on your heart,
bind me to your will,
that you and I won't part.

teach me your ways,
that I may worship you
bless me for my obedience,
God so just and true.
destroy my distractions Lord;
invade heart and mind.
revive me, Blessed Savior;
give me breath of life.

teach me your ways,
that I may worship you;
lead me with your hope and faith
in all I say and do;
lead me through the valley, Lord,
in your peace and grace.
teach this wayward child
to always seek your face...

IF HEAVEN HAD A RENTAL STORE

Hello good evening! Can you tell me if my Anya is here?
My loved one and darling!
All indicators, based on your narrative,
attest that she should be here, and I'm just asking if I can see her.
You'd like a better description? Oh you know her!
She was a stalwart for the Lord in every way, shape and form;
filled with integrity and didn't deviate from the wholesomeness of protocol.
She was tough in her love and did right by the people;
all she did was for the glory of God
'til she was taken up in the glory of God, my Anya.
Maybe you've seen her around, stern faced 'til that heart-warming smile
beaming bright melts your insides
and you see behind the seriousness, she's quite alright.

Maybe you've seen her sitting at the feet of YHWH
being amazed by the splendour of her Lord;
maybe you've seen her with balled fists giving glory and praise
with the Holy Ghost comforting her, as always.
Maybe you've seen my Anya, my dearly beloved whom I miss desperately,
not as much as her thirst for holiness.
But I miss her, can I, if need be, borrow her from you, even if it's for a few?
A couple hours to eternity is absurdly miniscule.
And I know you chose her–lived, suffered and died for her–
but she loved me, she challenged me,
and she did it for God and his glory!

May I just borrow her?
Tell me, what is it that you need from me for this to be a possibility?
How many ways must I tell you I miss her?
Because memories don't materialise
and dead bodies don't recite scripture
I'd just want to see her again, as I once did- without the pain
able to respond to her name- I'd want to hug her with life,
because after death it's no longer the same.
I know you don't change, but I'm asking for some slack
that I make look upon my sister and mentor for one more embrace
since her name isn't Lazarus and coffins don't hug back.
I've been struggling and coping with your decision
and it is fair for she is yours
but I miss her so much, since she left- all I have is this hurt.

But if heaven had a rent a center
I'd pay below the minimum as my interest grew
because it'll mean I'd get to spend more time with you.
If heaven had a rental store I'd work there
for the discounts and beg for the overtime.
I'd come in early for free just for a chance to see you be,
in glee as you tell me stories of you basking at Ancients of Days feet.

I'd take lunch breaks just to hear you speak
or see you play away this pain
that the cross didn't take away.
And if I should die- hopefully you taught me enough
for me to be seen as worthy by He that chose you
to by some measure of luck pick me
then I can learn from you
what you learned from Him for Eternity's eternity.

I miss you and I love you still,
and I wish heaven had a rental store...
because if it did, I'd be willing to match whatever miracles Christ did
just to see you smile or see you laugh like you once did.
Enjoy heaven for me,
if I never get a chance to make it there...

Destitute Diaries: Devoid One

I hope, above all else that I can hope for or with,
that peace may abound plentiful amidst the wars and strife;
I pray that unity grips us and with that same hope.
I still wish that the powerful potency and unbridled nature of love
lifts us and I hope that we would grow together,
aiding in the deficiencies among us three.
but there is a craving in my spirit and a deep desire in my soul
that's pushed aside in my mind, and I pray somehow unison can be made,
but hope is delayed, and no one comes to aid.
I am now hopeless ... for there will never be united peace amidst we three,
kings of our own ways, arrogant in our own estate
and I suffer for it immensely. unless we bridge the gap by slaying our egos
and setting aside our selfish ways to become united in love
and hope maybe then we can finally become our own heroes.
but I know better than to hope against consistency;
I am lost and destitute in Vagrant Alley because every turn
is circular on Derelict's Road, but I'll always come back
to this very same place, with tears running down cheeks
and dejection tattooed to my face.
I need a powerful unending, an unyielding source of strength.

El Olam, I am yours.
Save Me.

One Crown, One Sovereign Lord II

I am numb to your presence.
I pray, LORD, that you call me out of this slumber
and raise me out of this dreaded coffin—
this treacherous sepulchre of steady unrighteousness.
Humble me forcefully that I may revere you honestly,
grasp me before you, LORD
posture my bones to be in a constant state of obeisance.
Hear my pleas, LORD of all
for I find worth in you, there is joy in you
no good dwells in me, 'cept you declare it so.
Empty me that I may be filled with you
rid me of the disobedience which has me always undone.

Cleanse me of this stifling filthiness
which blots out the sincerity of my praise.
Maker of the deep, first cause of causes
to which all things react,
rectifier of all things broken; the course of peace and chaos
obey whatsoever you have instructed.
Grace and mercy blow peace and unity
in the cool of the breeze on your elect,
your holy justice floods us with
the truth of our deserved condemnation.
Breathe in me the hope of life
that can only come from an all-powerful
and the all-knowing eternal Transcendence.

Destroy me, blessed sovereign
render me a faceless, brainless and mindless body
always giving you the glory to you alone, my Sovereign LORD.
Render me useless for human use
and enable me to be a vessel of honor, solely for your purpose.
Cripple me for your glorious walk, dwell among my inward parts
usurping this nature that drives me to passion uninhibited.
Instill in me a God-delighting response,
I pray, asking that you constantly be the cause and remedy for my ruin.
Magnificent creator and author of all
emboss your glorious penmanship on my heart,
write upon me your holiness
and stain me with your mercy, encapsulate me in your love.
Erase my alarming transgressions, as they too stand in fear of you.
Relinquish the evil which has painted its disgrace
upon the mechanics behind my face ...
El Olam... I am yours, save me.

Doubt Chronicles: Part II

Dear Lord (is this how you do it?)
it's me again and I'm sorta confused.
I mean if you made me to be in a state of constant destitution
and surreal poverty and suffering, why create in me a yearning for better,
if all my efforts won't bring me anywhere? I mean, why make
all my positive moves forward be treadmill-like, but all my negative moves
bring me back like unforgettable memories? I work and I work while
my body is sacrificed for the livelihood of my family and my loved ones,
and even that doesn't help to meet the needs. I want to serve you,
I want to do right by you, but I don't know if you would do right by me.
I mean, everyone else that doesn't do the right thing, they get ahead
and they keep getting ahead but the promises you have for me are all after
I've suffered and died; am I dying to live in some bedazzled afterlife when it
seems like praising you goes hand in hand with my strife and you haven't
done enough to prove that you're alive. Isn't this the truth of how it's been?
It's all economics to you huh: dig first then pay later?
Wouldn't a fairer sacrifice for me be to do whatever I please for the sake
of my goals and outcomes at the detriment of a hereafter that's already in doubt?
I mean, isn't hell worth the happiness of my family and loved ones?
I mean, you did it. You had a goal, and you set everything up just to achieve it,
and didn't you go to hell for it? I don't know, I'm sorta in my feelings
at the moment; I'm not really myself. I think doubt rented me out
as a contortionist, and I'm bent all out of shape for no reason
that I can reason with ...
Am I yours?

Can you hear me?

Request For Worth

As a Christian, men will say that I am deceived, that I am foolish;
and with my intelligence I should be able to reason more sensibly than
to cower in such baseless avenues of comfort contrary to intelligence.
They will throw jeers and ridicule me for following what they call invalid,
illogical, and they have also concluded that it's senseless and childish beliefs in
fairytales. But I know that in the proper time, all will consult with proof
from eyes, belief in mind and conviction of the soul and follow whatever
menial belief men of intelligence have always and already demeaned.
Throughout the inception of doctrines, which of them at some point have
not been refuted or rejected- declared blasphemous or sacrilegious?
Which have never been debunked, cast aside or ignored? I respect my detractors,
naysayers and believers of another faith or mental conviction, for even
they unbeknownst will show forth the majesty and glory of God, and I am
thoroughly appreciative for their rebuttals, for it is their unrelenting
criticisms that will always compel me to truly search the scriptures.
I know that there is no thing and nothing inside of me that allows
me to be acceptable in Your presence, El Olam. I am weak, extremely frail,
fickle, wicked, stubborn, naive and indecisive. I realise all that I need,
all the necessities to be a proper follower of your word, do not lie in me,
but they completely reside within You. Faith is not mine, mercy is not mine,
love nor grace belong to me; but justice, yes, justice–that belongs to me.
The terror of wrath, the sweet euphony of gnashing teeth, the sound
and joy that is weeping in torment, now that is all mine.
None of the aforementioned gifts that were not mine are not mine
to lay claim to with confidence of any sort. Therefore, I do not find it
at all a laborious task or tedious chore to pick up my cross and to pick it up daily.
I glory in no thing and nothing inwardly that manifests itself outwardly,
for all that I desire cannot be mustered by my complete lack of necessities.
My needs are great and difficult to gain, for they are exclusive to you,
and those whom you've gifted according to the majesty of your sovereignty have them.
Here I am, willing (now, somehow) after much prodding and learning, through
searching and attempting to make practical the theories to serve you.
I have needs, Lord, none of which I can supply or find a supplier
with my deficiencies. I come to you for them, not to brag to other people,
not to make light of your mercy and grace. I have no intention of using
it to glorify things which you stand against biblically.
Give ear to a struggling servant who is unworthy to be in your presence;
I am asking for that which should enable me to be a better slave
and a better servant, according to your will and glory.
I count all things gain in you, even if the outcome does not suit
my presupposed and dream-built outcomes
that are tailor-made to my happiness. Here is my surrender; and as
I bow in sincerity. I hope to daily put my face before your feet in hopes
that you'll find me worthy to put your feet upon
my head and accept my surrender.
I surrender.
I am Yours. Save Me.

A Vagabond's Request (a song)

I have used your mercy
I have wasted your grace
I have come before you, Lord,
a total disgrace.
And I plead, before thee,
my God and my King.
Forgive my ev'ry sin
and cleanse me within, Lord,
Cleanse me within;
Cleanse me within Lord.
Cleanse me within.
CLEANSE ME, WITHIN.

THE LONG TELESCOPE

I often hear that God is all-knowing, that he knows the end from the beginning.
I also hear he sees all, and is in control of everything. Some say that God
is in the big things, others say he is in the details. Of course this is Christianity
we're talking about, so naturally every point has multiple sides that each individual
either knows, debates, denies or is oblivious to. But I keep hearing about this
telescope of time that God looks through and I'm perplexed and confused.
I usually hear it when people talk about his foreknowledge or his dealings
with the future ... it's said He doesn't know what we are doing or going to do
because we have free will, but he looks through this telescope of Time
and sees what we're doing and that's how he knows what we're going to do.
To me, the whole thing seems off. He's all-knowing, but only
because he can look ahead through some mythical telescope.
didn't understand the sense of the wording. Words have meaning,
and if they do, their meanings give way to context and understanding, no?
Why does he need a telescope to see through time? Didn't he create
time in Genesis? Wasn't he there before time existed?
Or was time, time before God, and gave him a telescope that he might see?

If God looks through the long telescope of time and the world is six thousand
or fifteen billion years old, does that mean he's short-sighted; if that's the case,
how short-sighted, a hint of astigmatism maybe? If he made everything
and still can't "see it through" because of how much time had passed, is
he short sighted and short-sighted? Are they saying God is myopic?
Who's his optometrist? Can God make a boulder he cannot lift?
Does he create problems he himself can not fix? Can God make something
and not see it? Does time play hide and seek with Him? Did time
break up with God? Is God a stalker or a peer? Wait a minute: did time
give him a trinket to remember her by, and anytime he misses her he looks
through the long telescope of time to see her? Let me get this straight:
God looks through this long telescope of time to see what's ahead,
so he knows what's coming?

When did he begin needing this telescope? Which bible character
can we track where the need for His telescopic vision initially began?
Here's a question: does vision of the telescope reach farther than his hands do?
Could it be true, and the unbelievers are right when they say h
ow can God see and not save? Does the God that looks through telescopes
have another God with the divine equivalent of twenty-twenty vision?
Does God have a God? Are there multiple
Gods based on vision and telescopes? This long telescope of time,
I couldn't understand it; I still don't. Is it a euphemism?
Is God going blind the more time goes on? Did he look ahead and see that
he was going blind? Wait, what does he use to look ahead with?
Was Lucifer mad because God didn't recognize him anymore?
Wait another minute: does the telescope need updates and upgrades?
So did everything come from God in the first place?
Wait, would that mean we were really made in his image?
Wait, is he eternally flawed? Is eternity the only thing that separates us?

Ugh, too many thoughts.

Let me settle down for a minute gather and my thoughts ...
Are they really saying that God needs this telescope of time to see what's going
to happen; doesn't that mean that he's contingent because his vision is waning or,
as the bible puts it, waxeth dim? Doesn't that mean he's dependent as we are?
Can you imagine a Pearl Vision in heaven? If there is a Pearl Vision,
do they have competition? As a matter of fact, are there other
businesses in heaven? Were the angels that got evicted part of the first Union?
Does heaven have a Better Business Bureau; wait, is heaven a metropolis
or is God a superhero and the devil just a nondescript mega villain?
Is heaven the first Batman story, the devil the first Joker? Wait, is Jesus Superman?
Is Martha Lilith? A Yellow Pages? Taxis? Where do we draw the line from
just a "telescope" and God's inability to see the fullness of his handiwork?
Is God's creation more perfect than his vision? Then, if his vision isn't as good
as his creation, whose vision did he use to create creatures
and whose eyes were used to say that everything he created was good?
I digress, unmissable irony; the all-powerful, all-knowing God
who's only all seeing with his incapacitating telescope...
Whose God is this? Not mine!

Destitute Diaries: Part II

Keep me, o Lord, from the end I've caused myself.
Steer me from the recklessness that would see me undone.
Straightway, I head toward catastrophe
and I am unable to find a solution to help myself.
I was unwavering in my displeasing you,
but here I stand, resolute in my demise,
but still in total need of you.
Help me, Lord...
Heal me, God, even though
I have yet to commit to you fully in obedience ...
Save me from the many
"I'm sorrys" and "please forgive me"
I'm seem to plague You with.
I'm sorry for being a disgrace before thee,
forgive me for the filthy rags
I've thought to be clean to wash your feet.

I am Yours, please save me.

One Crown, One Sovereign Lord III

My God, give keen ear to an object
that is the diadem of worthlessness.
Without you I am purposeless ... unending
Lo, without you I am brokenness unmended,
hopelessness extended.
Grant me you, whose mercy has select sinners befriended.
Count me worthy among the wretched blessed
Grant me the humility to accept what you've allowed
and grant me the right mind to seek you
in the glorious struggle sin transports.
No good thing have I to bring before thee to appease thy wrath,
but, Lord, gift mercy since no deeds have I, nor merit stored
to ask for anything other than what is fair.
With filth-brimmed lowliness I ask for grace,
though I am continually undeserving, perennially unworthy.
I am yours, save me; ruin me for the manifestation of your holiness.
Enable me to be obedient as the beautifully mindless things you've created.
Grant me the constancy of the sun to dwell in the truth of your word,
the loyalty of a rooted tree to abide always in the trusty foundation that is you.
Grant me the sensitivity of animals as they are perceptive of the times.
Grant me the indwelling of your Holy Spirit
that I may in all ways be aware of your presence
and keep me even more that I won't ever have to stray.
Grant me the wisdom of the of the rock rabbits
that you may be the rock that I dwell in to hide my frailty
Blessed Ancient of Days, who declares all things and they are so,
posture my bones to be in a constant state of obeisance.
Eternally hallowed is your name, even more sacred is your word,
commandeer my mind and force my surrender.
Empty me that I may be filled with you.
Overwhelm my mouth that my speech may speak of thee.

I am yours, save me.

Doubt Chronicles: Part III

Dear Lord
I'm sorry about that the last time.
It's just you don't really talk to me and I get it, I do. I'm a sinner,
and of the worst kind to begin with. Talking to me is pointless;
I don't know you and I don't play a part in your plan. What I want to know
is only on a need to know basis, and I don't need to know anything at all.
I could look to the Christians, but they sometimes don't even know
what they believe. And I was always taught to take it
from the horse's mouth and figured, hey, everybody talks to you;
why not join the fad? That's not even what I'm about,
but desperate times call for desperate measures, another earthly cliché.
I guess because I've been naïve about so many different things,
I won't allow myself to be completely naïve about you.
I mean, you're God, the creator of everything. I mean, if there was a big bang,
it was you who'd be able to tell us what it sounded like, or what it looked like,
or what you did to make it so great and so loud. They say you give
purpose to everything. Every success, every hurt,
all the bad and the good; they say that you transcend all our inferiorities
and deficiencies. Who else am I 'sposed to run to? Why don't you answer?
Will you answer? Will you keep ignoring me while I pour the heart
you gave me out to you? Is it not packaged right so the initial sender returns
it to the receiving sender? I need answers; I need you the way
you constantly ignore me. Maybe it's not you,
maybe there's someone bigger than you. Maybe I need to create something else
and give power to that. Maybe I shouldn't even discuss these things with you.
Maybe I should just share how I feel. I might be wrong,
I might be ridiculed, but it'll be honest. I'm tired of doubting, waiting,
crying, defending and explaining. I'll do what I feel I need to do...
whichever deity it reaches, I s'pose, will meet me wherever I go.

Outcomes: Part III

Here's a question: If there were no issues or problems in our lives,
would the praise be the same? Would your worship?
Or gratitude? If the outcome was always in our favor,
would we essentially need God or any god for that matter?
Does our insufficiency and constant lack of control force
us into acknowledging the one Being we pretend
to believe is in charge of everything? Are we consistent?
No? Do we change? Yes? Are we indecisive? Yes?
Do our prayers change? Yes? Does how we feel about ourselves
and our state of mind stay the same? No. We and our minds change,
our ideas change - our desires, and therefore our prayers change.
The many outcomes we desire also change;
however our (sin) nature doesn't change,
but the remedy of our state,
God, doesn't ... outcomes are God's work,
and all his work will be accomplished.
So regardless of the issues, the problems
and worries that come out of our life,
no matter the dislike of any particular outcome,
we as believers should always come out with intentional
and wholehearted worship in spite of whatever it is we experience.
Whatever His will for the outcome, our praise
and obedience should be ceaseless.
Forgive a vagrant finding his way, on Derelicts Road.

THE MIRROR

We are a train of reactions
in front of a revolting visage that is a supremely decrepit,
an undeniably filthy and grossly grotesque portrait of total despicability;
I am still, thoroughly infatuated with. This ever-decaying, miserable-minded,
presence-polluting, fad-hungry, categorically unstable, exhaustively incapable,
sensibly blind and yet emotionally potent to feel my way out of good sense right back
into the murky, guilt filled, pain full, regret permeating sinking sand
of failure and heartache. My dire worthlessness whose sum totality
is the accumulation of self-loathing and aweless self-disgust
on the other side of priceless;
in my opinion it is a spectacle worth the gawk.

A beautiful disaster, etched deeply in calamity, beautified only
in practiced oratory and the assurance of self-deceit. A structure rooted
in failure whose thoughts confirm the scaffolds now gone; unworthy
of any good thing; I kneel from before the actual mirror only
to be reminded by the poignantly vivid, descriptive images of my memory.
What a cursed resurrection! Turmoil masqueraded as excuses configure
a countenance that is a reproach unto itself. Is a convict encouraged
to continue in his err; are fools entertained outside the cause of teaching?
Why then must the destitute and hopeless be encouraged and given
reason to be optimistic in the methods and means which have produced
the result that they are so uncomfortable and dissatisfied with?
Why, must the proven incapables be allowed to be duped to believe,
that within them is the unearthed, well-spring of such magnitude
that would incredibly yet still assuredly make them...capable?

Alas fair mirror, whose truth is seen as a cruel commentator;
whose silence speaketh harsher words than enemies wholeheartedly bitter,
drowning in the grudges of ill-will and malice. Show me my cowardly state
that I may acknowledge, believe and be convicted convincingly about
the debt to error, I so desperately try to pay. Show me my state,
not the state of my imagination, or the plausible arrangements drawn
by my reality crippling creation primed by my fantasies. If being mean is a ruler
for honesty, I prefer constant cruelty. Fail not, even so when I,
embattled with the skewed priorities in my life forget to clean you
lest I justify my debilitating beliefs of inner goodness and strength.
Mirror, mirror do not fall short or become lax to grant me justice
for my ego tends to elevate me to the lofty heights of dismal depths,
impelling me to dwell in the disconsolate substratum
of disappointment and incremental sorrow. What hope have in myself,
when I have failed even in the joy and satisfaction of success?
What strength have I, in overarching weakness? Will faith grant me a miracle;
will the all-holy God look upon that which is unmistakably
a reproach and show mercy; a man can hope, can he not (smile)?

"Bondage Is For The Strong, Freedom For The Weak;
For freedom is bondage lying".

CAN WE PRETEND

I'm tired of trying too hard only to get nowhere;
I'm tired of complaining about things that ain't fair.
I pray and nothing, even my good deeds get spent
and I never did things for the reward but you'd think it'd help.
But if I'm born in sin, and you despise what ails me within,
how can I expect to win? So I propose that we just stop saying
we know each other and stop acting like we're friends
Since I know you won't answer then we might as well pretend.

So for starters
Can we pretend, that you answered all my prayers
before my loved ones got sick and died
that you provided solutions before my pillow-soaking cries?
Can we pretend you care, better yet, you hear?
Cuz you weren't there when the rent was due
and all the friends I sacrificed for started to act brand new.
I thought if anyone could, you would relate
but I don't know who was late more,
You or the day the rent was paid.
I gave my all for you, put it all on the line for you
Did whatever I could, whenever I could, listening to you
saying you'd show up knowing you never would.
Can we pretend you're real
and then act as though you care how I feel?
It can't be too much to ask,
compared to how much I've begged and grovelled
for you to see my plight from your divine bird's eye view.
Seriously, can we pretend like you care?
Pretend that when we hurt, your presence is near?
Cuz I'm all out of defence,
since your presence is merely a pretence
that I've been clinging on hopelessly
because of the miracles you used to share.

Can we pretend that the fasting and prayer
we've undergone for families and friends
didn't go unheard better yet unread
and that you were about to answer our prayer,
but you were interrupted?
Again can we pretend that all my health scares aren't serious
and I'm worrying for nothing cuz it's been a while,
and they say you're a punctual God
who operates perfectly through time,
but my body's deteriorating, my mind's dissipating;
is this a game we're playing? Here's your shot.
Why are you hesitating?
Please, if you're real, you don't have to prove it
to anyone else, just me.

Can we pretend like you aren't the mastermind behind every plight;
what was I thinking, like you'd honour my devotion
and struggle in this spiritual fight.
Wait, is it too late? If not, can we pretend again
that you are god and that I believe?
Cuz if you are, I haven't seen and I've been believing
I just think everyone's a better actor when they aim to be deceiving.
Can we pretend like we care about who we say we are
just for this instance and act like I don't love you
so we can justify our distance?
Can we pretend? I know it's your favourite game:
where we all act as though faith works and you'll keep your word.
But can we pretend like I'm a part of Israel
and you truly care, that way prayers don't really go on deaf ears.
Can we pretend to tell the truth for once
that you don't have purpose and the agnostics are right at least?
Because then our lack of knowledge plays into your plausible deniability.

We merely amuse you and that's all we're good for.
What is man that you are mindful of him
but clay in beleaguered cycle of amplified reruns,
diluted remakes of your past shows that have gotten old?
Can we pretend like you love us
and all these bibles stories are real?
Why do you want me here? Why do we go through so much?
Why don't you answer me? Why did you make me and leave me?
Why all these rules and chains?
Why do we play divine hide and seek
only for us to be the only participant in the game?
Are you here; do you care? Will you listen, don't you feel?
Can't you see?
Well, I guess until you do I don't know if I can continue to pretend
like you're real or that you're exist.
There's too much at stake and too much to fix.
I'm probably an unimportant vessel of dishonour with no use to you...
I don't even know why I wrote this
you've never answered even after all this time,
I guess by now I should be used to you.

Destitute Diaries: Part III

Guide me, oh Lord, for greatly my weaknesses abound,
overshadowing my efforts and my attempts to keep a firm hold on
what minimal glimmer of hope there be. Revive me, oh everlasting,
Everlasting; uproot my dual-minded reasoning and allow me
to be solely one way of obedience,
for it is difficult to steer my will there myself.
Take the reins and lead me through each test,
that i may testify; lead me through the great obstacles,
that i may be grateful for providence.
Guide me, for without you i am lost.
Love me, for without you i am broken; free me, my God,
for my mind holds me captive.
Save me. i die daily with or without you,
but i need you immensely,
as i desire to die with your love
being the only albatross of my life.

oh God, save me;
i am still, yours...

Just Remind Me

Who do I complain to? When life decides to once again
put me between a rock and a hard place. Cause this ain't safe...
So which ruler do I seek to speak to, face to face,
about the calamities and the subtle injustices
that have so frequently taken place?
You see, I'm in pieces because I'm broken once again,
but this time beyond recognition
because the pieces of the pieces of me aren't even at peace.
They won't even come together peaceably to find peace with me;
that's why I've never, been whole.

For years, I've not only been broken,
left without hope and unable to cope with
the misery from my shame and failure;
I've been beat down, then depressed and stressed.
I'm saying, God, with all due respect,
can you please do this son you made a favour?
Because I'm tired of being disappointed
and left without hope to find.
All these hours I work, and all the money that comes
goes quicker than the blink of an eye,
I'm caught between the pain of a bad decision
and the inhumanity of a worse choice all at the same time.
I'm trying to starve more, to help my kids starve less,
these are just some of the daily cruelties
that repeatedly plague my mind,
and you have the nerve to ask for yours, God?
Well, I just wanna know, where's mine?

I'm sorry, Lord. (deep breath) please forgive me.

I just need a break, Lord, from all the heartbreak!
Put brakes, Lord, on everything,
because all I see are pathways that lead to complaints, Lord.
Plus I'm trying to refrain, Lord, from being so ungrateful,
but the pain in me is painstakingly overwhelming,
and I'm honestly thinking about failing, Lord,
but with heaven and hell on the scale,
what's at stake is too great...
What I'm trying to say is that I'm still in this broken state,
hoping you would still give this wretch a face to face.
I just need you to remind me of mercy
because all this justice
has me desperately looking for grace...

And I know I'm a disgrace, Lord, but here I am,
no longer afraid to lay prostrate on my face, Lord.

Oh G-d, lest I forget again,
just remind me... that the all-powerful
sovereign God is He who designed me...
Remind me
that it was you who looked beyond my faults and saw me...
Remind me, that it was you who sent your Son to die,
from the worship in the heavenly stories,
and if that fails to register, remind me that the baby Jesus
we so easily joke about went from gory to glory.
Remind me that I have been pressed
on every side but not crushed. Remind Me,
that I've perplexed but was never in despair. Remind Me,
that I may have been struck down but I am not destroyed,
I may have been persecuted but was never abandoned.
Remind me, as I tend to forget
that you never left because you were always... right beside me.
Dear God if you love me,
fail not to lovingly remind me.

One Crown, One Sovereign Lord IV

Forgive me of the inherited nature that I emblazon.
Worthy is the lamb slain before the foundation of the worlds
in you do I find hope magnified and love personified.
Clothe my thoughts with the potency of your most holy decrees.
I desire to cling to thee even in times of strength
for pride is an ever-present response within my inward parts.
Harvest in me the desire to delight in that which you delight in.
Create in me the yearning to seek and dwell in your holiness.
Cause me to glory in the omnipotence of the sovereign LORD
Your will is established in all the earth
and no other instruction with they follow.
All things worship when you move,
the worlds shudder at the thought of you.
Grant me peace if it be in your will.
All that you have declared for me, cause me to accept graciously
with the same response of sincere thanksgiving.
The life I live is the offering table where
I'll daily offer myself prayerfully as a worthy sacrifice.

Forever just and righteous are the only eyes
who see all in its proper context,
Thou who knoweth all my shortcomings and ill-conceived motives.
Weigh my intentions, look past my crippling infirmities,
force my surrender; weaken me that I may search in thee for strength.
Be my every all and all in everything.
Blind my eyes to my abilities and desires
allow me to desire that which is insatiable with human effort.
Attack my ego with the truth of holiness
that I may never forget that you are the only sovereign in existence.
Give ear to a worthless bondservant
only desiring to give glory to the only target for whom glory matters.
All praise and honor, glory and dominion
To El Olam who reigns and does what he pleases
In heaven and in earth, in the seas and all deep places.
Blessed be you name and forever reign
for there is only One Crown, One Sovereign, the Holy LORD of all.

may it be so...

Welcome To
Grammerlin Square

Home of
The GrandmentalStation

All Aboard
The Grandscendence

Next Stop:

The Heart of A Man

What is beauty?
Is it defined before it is comprehended or before it can be appreciated?
Is its definition a meager execution to soil what we can't aptly describe?
Even with all the words, don't we fail to give an exact description
of the majesty we're continually faced with?
Is beauty solely the image of a thing, or is it in the purpose?
No matter how convinced we may be about our subjective idea of beauty,
truth is, it isn't exclusive to just a view.
It can also be found in the resilience to take a beating
and not lose hope or sight or perfection of what it loves to do,
and make no mistake: whatever it decides to do is intrinsically beautiful.

The heart of a man dares against the odds and damages, against
the hurtful beatings, the catastrophes and disappointments
to still soar as high and even higher, in spite of what was previously done.
It dances amidst its demise and smiles seeing
the impending doom and steps toward devastation
as though it revels in the gloom. This heart is a kite seeking no form
of refuge or means of rescue amidst a bevy of lightning sightings.
Fully aware of the tragedies, it moves soulful and free, vulnerable,
yet bold enough to bleed hope and resiliency.
Therefore, every heartbeat is greater than the pain it receives,
greater still than the pain it retrieves from the memories
it re-sees when the damage doesn't recede.
It still beats, maybe a second slower or a thump less; regardless,
it dances back and forth, to and fro, as strong and as wild as the hairstyle.
It prances about, wiggling through danger
and pussyfooting calamity with unadulterated glee.

It isn't naive nor oblivious, it just responds to a higher,
more profound call to be whole,
whether the object is mutual in its sacrifice or not.
It'll die for love before it'll die for self, and who they'll die for,
they'd live for a thousand times with only one life.
This heart ... bleeds undeserved second chances
and hopeless romantic because whether the choice
is to live for love or die for it is merely a matter of semantics.
This beating thing, destined to take a beating still,
cursed to be relentlessly passionate while it doles out
unrequited pumps of forgiveness, and in spite of the events it faces,
its stance never changes; even when the pain contorts
and it dances awkwardly, it dares to love wholeheartedly,
while the return is unarguably partially.
This heart of this man, though tattered, smiles—
though fragile, still wild.
Truth is, this heart's beat,
but still... beats...

If I Could Spit Game

I don't spit game, but if I did maybe sound like this:
I am not worthy in any way, shape or form
to appreciate the magnitude of beauty that you are...
You are absolutely a rare prize,
from the unbelievable amazingness
that permeates from the wellspring of your insides
to the dazzling glimmer of heaven
that manifests awesomeness every time you candidly smile.
(sigh, your smile)

I'd wage countless wars with each and every flaw
and schedule random interventions with all my faults
just to remind you who you are and will be to me:
a queen, whose throne is my heart, body and my mind,
used at your whim because I was forged
before the usher in of time to fit your life's design,
and your life's design is for you to smile.
(sigh, your smile)

And though the weather's never always pleasant,
because sometimes we drown in our own sorrow and misery,
still, I'd swim through the hottest hells and highest heavens,
daring against all herculean impossibilities,
just to make sure I make shore every time.
To assure you and remind you that if you're here with me
I'd make wherever we are our paradise.
I gaze at you, losing sight of everything
but my subdued confession of love for you.
(sigh. I'd be the greatest love to you)
And I'd never regret what I'd give up for you

I am in love with being in love
with the hidden and unappreciated parts of you
that you hide because it makes you
so self-conscious and uncomfortable,
I'd love a chance to love you every chance I get...
(sigh. I'd be the greatest lover to ever love you)
But I don't spit game I'm awkward in love, clumsy and smitten,
because around you, I uncontrollably mumble and fumble...
So until I get the confidence to approach you
I'll walk the scenic route, away from you,
admiring everything that the gods
took pleasure in as they designed you.
Thinking about all the things I'd tell you
without ever telling you... like I was only meant for you,
and my purpose on earth is to live and die loving you.

(I wonder if she can read minds)

The Misappropriation of Now: Part I

The truth of the matter is, we all have time; yes, all of us; however,
not in equal shares, as some live longer than others.
What we do share in abundance, if you've lived some, is now.
Yes, I know it seems so random or peculiar identifying now with abundance.
Fact is, until you're dead, you're running on, or with,
a seemingly unending and seamlessly unappreciated series of nows.
Yes, even now. Now is one of the greatest tools we possess,
and yet we continually fail to make use of.
It converts and bridges time, present and future into the past.
The past was now, the present is, and the future will be.
The inevitability of now is unrelenting.
The problem that we have with it is that it's usually not as beautiful
or as grandiose or as spectacular as the future.
We are so enamoured with the possibility of what it may hold
that we fail to make use of the fundamental building block
that all future is built on: now.

Words Escape Me: A Letter to Love

If only I could find the exact words to speak...
Bear with my struggle

"'There be no other love that's even worth the search;
you're my ever after, my joy of laughter, I am forever yours.'"
I love you, beyond good judgement and measly sentiments,
beyond overplayed clichés and the overly mushy PDAs
that all new couples display...

I want to ... love you with a love that surpasses
whatever limits of love that were shown to you.
I aim to give you the love that you dreamed about
or saw in movies but appeared to you as elusive
or not conducive to the life you live.

(I'll say it slowly, so you hear it) I... love... you...
I need a lifetime in a lifetime beyond a lifetime
in an eternity beyond eternity to love you dearly,
more dearly than a mother's first touch to her infant son,
a father's delicate eyes and tender heart
towards his forever sweet baby girl.

I intend to love you better, in a span that doubles forever,
etching our love in the annals of history
with no thought of making history,
so long as loving you is my only misery.
(though impossible, you're worth every attempt)

I plan to love you amazingly, with new memories of laughter
that'll last throughout the ages, a legacy of love that'll have our kids
rereading our love letters of actions in our united pages.

I love you (plain and simple)

And your smile, the smile that intoxicates my mind
and forces my eyes to look away as I fail to blush in secrecy saying...
She can't be mine, but I'm grateful you are,
for your presence soothes my busy mind...
And as you whisper "come back to me,"
I'm reminded that I've been blessed with a gift that never gets old.

A gift that never ceases to bring hope,
a gift so valuable, priceless shies away, costly bows in humility.
You are mine and mine forever more.
I live to love and love to live life in love with you forever more.

I love you (and I still will)

With unsaid words, but actions that speaks leagues,
this maybe best explained in soccer terms,
you see, but I love you more completely
than the bitter hatred between inner city rivalries...

I just wanna love you with actions,
stink of sincerity and integrity and defiled by truth.
I commit to you my all, as flaws mangle my human frame,
there be no better dame with whom I'd share my name
and sing lullabies of bliss while the stars
unite with Mother Nature for Love's refrain...

and though words escape me,
I will forever right the wrongs done to you with love...
and though the words fail,
I'll forever write my heart to you...
in love

I Love You
(I truly do, and though these words escape me,
this is the best I could do...
(I'm so sorry if this wasn't good enough)

DEAR DIARY

May I clench jaws in hands
and intently search for the galaxy of love in your eyes?
May I hold you again, but this time, with more purpose?
I'm sorry, as I allowed ego to let separation hurt us,
I miss all that we used to be.
Come back to me, because I'd lovingly squeeze you,
meanwhile listening diligently
for the sound of heaven in your heartbeat.
I'd set pride aside just to win your heart,
I'd place it down on every puddle in life
just so you can comfortably walk across.
Dear Diary, do you think they'd believe me if I told them
that my love is like
the brightest sunrise on the darkest days
or that on those darkest days when you don't see my rays,
I'd be right here to show you I need you in a million ways?
Reason eight hundred ninety-five thousand two hundred and fifty three:
I need you to know that inside of me
is the divine blueprint of love, affection and passion
that can wrap you up in bliss for an eternity.
You are the greatest gift for me and I present you with you,
for in presenting you with you
there's undoubtedly more of you all for me.

Dear Diary,
Do you think they would sit and forget about time?
As I attempt to explain away my complicated feelings,
rambling incoherently about how the most absolute
mathematically logical rule states
no (x) can equal (y) I have and will always love (u).
(Did I say I love you? sigh)
May I hold your hands 'til sweat begins to form
'til separate bodily fluids unite and tell how
we were meant to be before our parents' parents were ever born?
I miss you; I miss seeing how biteable lips contort
as your mouth metamorphs from sexy smirks to geeky laughter.
I miss saying I love you and calling you my happily ever after.
May we kiss once again, 'til we become tongue tied
and bound by the language of love and passion?
Would you believe me if I told you
I love us in every which unfathomable way;
would you believe me
if I told you that loving you is just as painful
as staying away?

Dear diary, am I in denial?

Work of a Man's Hands: Worth the Love

I Love YOU...

More than breath-taking adjectives can describe,
more than divine verbs could execute,
and more than every special and rare noun, past present and future tenses.
Whatever the predicate is, I will bear all in corny parts of speech;
grammatically speaking, I hope you enjoy these loving life sentences ...
I'm willing, beyond discomfort and unusual occurrences,
to set the ego of an arrogant young boy aside
and be the faithful man you deserve ... not just because I want to,
BUT BECAUSE IT'S RIGHT.
Will you allow superimposed failure to love you with all his imperfections
deemed unbearable by the masses who don't know him?
Would you allow failure to disrobe and show you the passion in his love,
the fire in his heart and the sincerity in his touch?
I love you ... and though calloused my hands be,
they'll forever be gentle, as I hold your cheeks
and plant kisses on your forehead
'til smiles stain and last longer than the life of great oak trees.

I ... Love ... You...

beyond the insecurities keeping a watchful eye over your progress
(YOU GOT THIS)
and though it hurts me when I saw you settle for mere rocks and stones,
it doesn't make me love you less ... you're still a gem
(always have been), revalued after it switches hands;
the previous appraisers, who ended up losers,
didn't know better when they misused you, abused and refused you,
and I know it's been hard, but I wanna re-establish the faith
you had in yourself before the world razed you.
I wanna double the love tenfold that you're parents used to raise you,
and give you the love, butterflies and giggly smiles
that fairy tales and happily ever afters gave you ...
I'm not promising perfection; I'm offering a sincere effort
to be a dependable man for whatever blow life swings;
I promise to stand in front or beside you when you hide or face your fears
and to use my hands as impromptu kerchiefs to wipe your tears...

Did I forget to mention, that I ... love You;
and I pledge allegiance to your every all,
to love you more than the painful memories
of past heartbreaks that taint your heart.
May I show you how loving you in truth
can break down the fortress from which you need rescue?
I want to love you longer and hug you
tighter than desperation's strangle hold;
assuring you that you're safe and promise I won't let go...

I don't know if this love is possible, but
I love you, and I wanna be the man that you can run to;
the pair of arms that won't ever push you away
but'll always embrace you, hold you, pick you up and protect you.
I'll cherish the moments when we can't help but smile,
when stomachs manufacture soul-fluttering butterflies,
and the depth of love is felt without touch and seen in the eyes.
I'm grateful that, come what may, we took a chance on love,
and took a chance to love, found a chance to breathe,
a chance to be special and a chance to see,
that love, when real, goes beyond boundaries,
and that a love that's real will always form new memories

I Love You.

Love in U Major – Loving You Major

I declare that, above all that may matter
within the depths of my fluttering heart,
to love you wholeheartedly, and to never take any time apart.
I love you, amidst the flurry of self-proclaimed flaws
that sets your brand and value of amazing light years afar...
Just know that
you (alone) are my AMAZING with a love so profound,
I actively laze in ...
May I (please) rest here (in your heart, soul and mind) alone,
'til coffin and maggots occupy a body once riddled with
bloody organs and a divine love jones.
This, my dear, be my solemn hope

because

I love you, in a major way,
and for that I'd freely give you all of me,
in spite of the necessity of the parts of me;
I would eternally give to thee the very last of me,
(just to see you smile).
Oh, that smile, whether it be true or in defense,
I'll love you, even when you're lined up in the protective sequence
of a happy pretence, I'll love you still with all truthfulness...
offense or defence, I'll be here with the same jersey,
willing to aid you with hugs and sincerity for the win,
for no losses abound here, so long as I'm tied you.
I'm all for you, because of you (just to remind you)
that I was created solely to love you...
That therefore is the pinnacle of all that I can do;
I do nothing better than to do love, true love,
with every single part of you
and why, you may ask again
well, have I ever told you that you're worth it?

Well, in case I forgot,
you're worth it–so worth it, more valuable
than the most invaluable pricelessness sold constantly.
Won't you be mine to hold, with a non-refundable constancy?
May I take the time to show that I will and do love you honestly?
Honestly, with my love as my witness,
witness that you are skiing on the forefront of my mind, regularly
and for that I'm grateful, that God set you apart in His grace for me,
and for that, I will undoubtedly love you
in every major way, without change,
on the bad, important and not so special days...
I'll cherish you, hold you; all I can bring myself to do
is loving you in a major way.

COMPLETE ME

Would you mind if I asked for you
to complete me, against the wiles of pride
that tell us to hide the perfection of a bond
that permeates the recesses of our minds?
Would you complete me
if we had to gather the jagged remnants
of our most painful and deepest secrets
with hands bloodied by the search
for the cure of our growing weaknesses
just so we could find wholeness
in the misery of our broken pieces?

Would you dare, if comfort was sacrificed
and you were ridiculed by skeptic eyes
who doubted that our love would
ever rise above the hope of their smiling lies?
Would you still dare to complete me
even if it went against everything that you believed,
clouded every judgement you had so you couldn't see,
but you're helpless against
the unshakeable feelings you can't help but feel?

Would you, if you could, complete me
with mistakes and potential in tow,
travailing in love wherever the faults
of our affection compelled us to go,
even if we were hand in hand,
journeying away from states of hurt
to happiness is distant lands?

I love you with the most profound reason
any mere mortal could find—
a reason so drenched in love
it would convince
Christ to forgo his destiny to die—
and find purpose in life...
but even so, would you
complete me, if your broken heart
needed my broken heart to survive,
but we had to swap hearts
as often as possible, lest we die?
Would you try? To make what you think
is impossible work?

The Misappropriation of Now: Part II

We become Picasso, Rembrandt and da Vinci at painting a future we,
at the time of the drawing, are intentless in manifesting.
All we have is now; all we can afford is now.
See, everything can happen now
the very same way it can happen in the future.
Fortune, misfortune, good and bad.
But we are so enamoured and mesmerized even,
maybe because we are so miserable in our nows
that we catapult our subconscious into imagination overload
so we can work towards the future to appease our misery.
Truth is, now is the building block of the future;
we don't see it as such because we operate in the future tense.
All of our current efforts are now empty but future-filled.
No real work towards the future, except hail mary prayers,
and going for the gusto hopes.

Work of a Man's Hands: Idle Fingers

May I hold you? Gently ... intently, yet ever so softly
by your neck and jawline? I need to
look squarely in the heart of your eyes ...
smile and kiss your forehead as though my kisses
would transform the very DNA of love
that floats within the secret parts of your mind ...
Is that fine? Would you like? I'm just curious; baby, may I?
I wanna tell you I love you ... with no words or speech,
just by spontaneous neck and back rubs,
cooking amazing man sandwiches, and as you eat,
I'd yell out reasons why "you're my amazing"
and write why you're the best part of having lungs to breathe
all while my thumbs rub away
the pain of a hard work days from your feet.
Would you let me, maybe kiss your feet,
and hug with warm hands every toe individually?
Would you smile? Can I try? Baby, may I?
I'm beyond impressing you with ulterior motives;
I'm not here to confuse you;
I'm just trying to show you the image of a man
unlike you're used to, hidden behind the wall
of extraordinary and usual disappointments
that have repeatedly abused you.
I'm just trying to show you that you deserve
the divine, hand-sculpted perfection of flaws that compliments
perfectly your every trait.
You've held your breath in hopes of finding the real;
baby, I wanna be the reason you exhale.
Would you mind? A sigh of relief?
You deserve it. baby, just breathe.
I'm merely showing that you are worth knowing...
I see immense worth in you, and I value your total being
and not just the partial views
that have gotten you rave reviews by shallow dudes
who never really had your best interests at hand.
I'm saying, if I didn't just tell you, but proved to you,
would you hold my hand?
Just hold on; your heart and mind are safe in my hands...
I really want to slow dance to the skips
of your heartbeats on the beach, surrounded by loved ones
wearing our favourite colours and holding candles...
And maybe as I'm dancing, whispering proven vows in your ear,
you'll feel the sincere love I have for you, and the desire to be your last.
I'd get on bended knee and ask, if you don't mind,
sharing fries and annoying commercials through classic movies
for the rest of our lives.

SNOOZING: FRAGMENTED MEMORIES

It's late, and you're tired from long days and longer nights,
and still, for another year, you are still a most breath-taking sight.
While you sleep, I become the most loving creep,
as I count and multiply the blinks of your eyes
and the amount of times you breathe.
I sit up awoken from the incessant alarms that you chose to snooze.
Now here you lay, late, as I fix our one and only her breakfast plate.
We'd sing her favourite songs and do our favourite dances,
her heart so pure, her mind so pure.
She reminds me so much of you.

Now I'm reminded of you,
so I send Love in your direction;
to do what I chose not to do—
for how could I interrupt Gods vision
of perfection, in perfect slumber too?

Most days I just lay there, immobilized by your closed eyes
as you are immortalized in my very life.
[Inhale and exhale]- your very breath is the reason
this journey of love set sail.
Your being is the sole reason why love will prevail.
My ever after and my amazing sleeps in peace,
breathing queenfully as she feels for me.
I reach out to her consciously,
while I subconsciously meet her soul's greet,
and this has been our resting retreat and our rest and repeat.

I tell you a thousand times I love you, and I mean it a million more.
I can name everything I love about you when you breathe,
have I ever told you I see eternity in your eyes whenever you sneeze;
I mean I see the universe with possibilities in a world of impossibilities.
I love you, and as you lay, ignoring as many alarms as you choose,
I send my love as I send our Love to wake you up from your slumberous snooze.

Baby girl, it's time to wake up Love!
What do we say?
"Hi, mom! It's time to wake up, Love."
"MOM, mom! Dad says it's time to wake up, Love.
So, mommy, wake up, Love."

The Masterpiece: BeholdHer

YOU were sculpted by the hands of the divine,
the manifestation of a flawless blueprint
masterfully constructed in the majesty of a beautiful mind.
Therefore, you ARE the showpiece
He intended for you to be, before the frailties
you project were stored on the hard drive of your mind.
And in spite of the incessant nagging of your deficiencies,
you are MY masterpiece and my BELOVED rarity;
from the visibility of your gums or the minor gap
that your laughter uses as an amplifier; I love all that.
Truth is, YOU'RE more than your spontaneous giddiness,
more than the odd timing of your serious tone and hilarious silliness.
A good woman, hidden behind damages no one ever cared to address;
I'll show you that you're worth being loved,
even if you can't see PAST your cluster of regrets.
You are more than what you see, leagues beyond what you know—
a superb assembly of amazing, never seen by earth before.
And regardless of the flaws or issues
that you believe tile the beauty of God that you continually downplay,
I'll be here to prove to you that you are worth
every masterstroke his PERFECTION displays.
I'll FOREVER be your historian,
giving the guided tour of your epic wonderfulness;
sharing the blatant evidence of how rare you are,
proudly telling those who never got to experience
the survival story of every scar and the blessing of every flaw.
You aren't my creation, but I'll be your restorer;
bringing back the stunning beauty you used to share;
with loving hands, I'll remove stained tears
that have prevented you from seeing clear.
I'll be steady and gentle hands that HOLD you above your impairments
when you've been backed into a canvas of your fears.
Even when YOU try to hold it together with unease,
you can never hide behind the cracked lines of unbelief.
I understand seeing yourself is hard for YOU to do, but it saddens me
that you don't see the true value of your unparalleled beauty.
Better yet, it pains me to see you unaware of your worth; what's worse is
you compare your hurt, from tragedies to well-dressed lies,
because your eyes can't see past the makeup of internal demise.
You ARE a worthy prize, not to be compared
to the inner turmoil and undetected deterioration that all replicas hide.
You are MY Mona Lisa, and we may not know why
that woman smiles, or if in the darkness of museums she cries.
But just as you compare all that passes you by in the streets,
preoccupied by the bogus fragilities you upkeep,
you may have been everybody else's common debris,
but you alone, will forever be
My MASTERPIECE...

Augustine's Affliction

These days, they simply don't have much left
as I've wasted energy and youth
on things that I've recently realised
have been utterly meaningless.
But for a chance to love deeper
than the heartbreaks seen, even with
these debilitating legs facing irreparable injury,
I'd run to you, fiercely,
as though each heartbeat
is a trophy not yet won.
I'd still run, even if spaceships didn't exist
and the distance to run is from Neptune to the Sun.
I'd sprint still, with every ounce of everything to give
racing the earth's orbits, facing predicaments,
disguised as longitude and latitudinal lines
just to ask if you'd mind taking a stroll
through the expanse of my love for you in miles.

(May I Step to You)

With open arms, dishevelled by karma's
wear and tear, may I hold you, through
loudest laughs and sincerest tears?
I'd hug you 'til muscles form hearts
and arms refuse to part,
for it's my desire to imprint on you
my hugging frame
so even if I'm not there, you'd experience
my warmth and smell just the same.
And with these hands, whose fingers fail
to maintain any good fortune they come across,
all that I've held trying to force love,
I have fumbled for great loss.
Yet it's as though this moment before the creation
of the worlds had been predestined;
for unknown reasons fingers put aside malice
to come together just so they can grab hold,
of this beaten thing...

(I Know It Isn't Pretty, But Here, It's My Best)

This heart that's been battle tested and love scarred,
cursed, with more Band-Aids than blood vessels,
and stuck by larger thorns that drew
more blood than the one Christ adorned—
My heart hasn't been whole since daddy broke it,

but for you, I'm compelled
to play hide and seek for the absent piece,
painfully fragmented by an absentee.
Truth is, I need this to be truly complete
so I can give you my heart with all its pieces,
perpetually, though not duct tape free.
Here's my best, my love, damaged and whole
for you ... to have and to mould,
would you mind keeping it safe even after we get old?
But before you choose, would you
still want me, as I am not cheap?
Would you still desire to love me the same
if unending streams of scattered tears
and yearly disappointment
was the total upkeep?

(Would You?)
Would I still be worth your time,
worth the weight of the migraines I could possibly,
though subconsciously, gift your peaceful mind?
Faced with the decision of for better or worse,
would you love me past the many times
I'm likely to get on your nerves?
Would you believe me if I told you,
that I'd love you with every deficiency found?
And I'd gather the sum of all that I lack,
only to have them bound,
and with the power and patience
it takes for pearls to be made,
I'll turn all of the disappointments from
disastrous hurricanes to partly cloudy days ...
I have no promise of perfection,
but I can promise you effort.
I've learned however you define love, you'll suffer it—
and for a lifetime with you, I'll suffer for free
If you'd love me and love me expensively, without receipts.

The Gathering of a Man's Hands

I see a queen, suppressed by the cheers for bad b!tches and dime pieces;
masquerading, degrading visuals for flightless buzzard to lustfully feast on.
I see you ... past the barbie images and dolled up mechanics
used to beautify the mighty insecurities and their militant defences.
I see ... past the masked smiles and forced laughter,
through battered and bruised heart that you...
are more than your defensive pretences...

(YOU)
I see you... past the baggage you simultaneously carry
with the hopes of being a better woman than your mother was.
I'll pick up the dreams that collided with worthless sacrifices,
repay the costly prices of love you were forced to pay.
I'd renew the determination in you that dwindled
because you were swindled by the pleasure-seeking cookie monsters
that only managed to be substandard men
who could never muster the wherewithal
to bring out and love the good woman in you...

(YES. YOU.)

I envision... it'd take more than poetic words to undo the many slurs
hurled by people who'd love to keep you at your worst...
and I know that fact hurts, but I'd only raise my hands
to peel back the lies that have formed thick layers of s'posed truth around you.
I'd show you that your beauty is real and ought to be seen!
It'd be poetic justice, when I strip the labels of hoe, slut and b!tch,
because you're more than what most men see!
They'd have you settle for subservient positions, doing as they please;
I'd merely gather the lost pieces of the puzzle
so you can see, from the beginning, you were only meant to be...

A WHOLE PARADIGM SHIFTING QUEEN!
(YOU ARE ...)

Let me, even if it pains or causes me to bleed,
pick up the fragmented fragments of broken dreams
beneath your feet that re-trample the shards of broken hearts
that continually get shattered— the same pieces that batter and tatter the feet
you still find strength to forge on despite the many tragedies
you hoped would've turned out better... I find it a worthy task
to sweep you off your mangled and tired soles.
let me attach and transform the jagged chunks of bitterness,
too incapable of being happy and whole on their own...
it's not an easy task I know... just know... that you...

ARE NOT ALONE!

The Perfect Love Story

Tell me, have you ever stood
with your knees buckling from your worst fears.
Unsure of what next will happen
so the substance of your manhood
is found only in tears? I'm scared; would you be?
If you were standing before your wife,
who's incredibly amazing, a woman whose heart
outshines every galaxy on any night.
But here she lies, doing what she can
with all her might, and for once, her all
isn't good enough to win this unfortunate fight.
I don't ask for much, but if you're up there, big guy,
send me a sign, and if I'm too hurt
to see the glimmer of hope
I'm just asking if you could please...

TURN BACK THE HANDS OF TIME

Turn it, just turn it back past the abbreviated
and short responses of love,
because we too often took each other for granted.
Now I'm frantic, hoping that whichever
deity is strongest above will
let me take back every unkind word
and partial hug because the day was bad
and the mood wasn't right. Turn it back,
so I can love you again, but this time I'll love you
twice as hard as the tattered Christ
was crucified before he was without life.
I know I can't, but if it involves loving you
it's worth the try ... Impossible never seemed
so impossible 'til now, since all
I'm strong enough to do is hold your hands and cry...

I CAN'T TURN BACK THE HANDS OF TIME

But if I could, I'd hold hostage father time,
and force him to continually press rewind,
just because I miss the hope in your eyes,
the brilliant sunrise in your smile;
even your tone of voice in your unending rants
and the unmistakable sarcasm in your sighs.
I fell in love with you heart first and was all in
because love makes you do stupid things
like forget to breathe and forget to think,
forget to eat, and learn to sing.
it makes you learn to hold, and learn to kiss,
makes you take for granted and learn to miss ...

The Hands Aren't Turning, But...

I'm hoping hard, but praying
with more passion than the Son did in the garden
because I can't accept this reality that shatters me.
Denial grips me, the truth rips me
and I'm too afraid to tell your number one fan,
her hero's losing, so I tell her
it's nap time and mommy's only snoozing.
Please, big guy, I'm begging you!
Take back the seconds moving forward
and the regrets piled high; take back the excuses
that line up in my mind in single file.

Turn back the hands of time,
even if it means you would never be mine;
I'd learn to remember you in the deepest
depths of my soul and in the unseen
and unreached crevices of my mind
because I can't go on knowing
that the greatest being next to Christ was mine
died and I never loved her
the best I could while she was alive... (sigh)
"Hey you, come here, baby girl, it's alright;
Please, baby, don't cry, mommy's only snoozing.
We just can't wake her up this time.

LIAR: The Introduction

We are gathered here today,
some to revisit love and others just to dive.
Please note that we are not responsible for your destination.
It is randomized; if you do decide to continue,
know that we do not control your beginning.
And once you begin, you and only you
control your movement until you land.

We do not account for weather,
and we don't care for your sob stories
or your ideas for revenge or ideals for revolution.
You are just another one, another number
who seeks hope or closure; don't forget, it will get tedious;
you will want to give up.
Hope will dwindle as you go on;
you can fall or cease to be.
It matters not, as you will at some point cease,
whether with us or in oblivion.

So for some of you,
this might be your first commencement speech,
for others, the thousandth, millionth, even the last.
Some of you will see the world for the first time; others, again.
Regardless of your status,
fall or fall no more, begin again or end again.
It is your option to go on through the mundane
the difficult, and the despair.
This is your chance to seek impossible,
find it and make it unneverable.

Welcome to this, your end of a new beginning
or a beginning to a familiar feeling;
dive or die again.
Welcome to the end.
There is hope and there is also the end.

LOVE IN A RAINDROP: THE FALL

My yearning is yearning, the ultimacy of intimacy.
What is my desire? It is the longing to love again
and to touch Love, to breathe in and absorb love.
To be conquered and overwhelmed by you,
forcing nature against its will to just be a drop on you.
The gods asked what would I want to be,
and it was there I decided, after inhaling death's cold oxygen,
that if reincarnation be an option,
I'd want to be the favorite thing of my love.
(abrupt stop)

I'd dream of being a single raindrop in a thunderstorm,
that though they maybe be wet, maybe LOVE can distinguish
my touch amidst a bevy of foreigners ingraining their wet DNA on my body:
The body I cared for, and gave my all, marred by past loves and crushes.
I fall in love to fall on love, screaming out for my baby to remember me.
Remember me and how gently you were caressed;
remember the smile I brought after I took sunrise
from distant time zones only to see dusk and dawn glimmer in your eyes.
Falling still, and falling all over again
with my lover and my favorite friend,
dodging other dare-fallers who just fall
over and over again because they never lived.
I plunge into hopes that whenever I land,
my love would have sensed the weather coming
and searched for me like gold at the end of every rainbow,
but it'd be in every thunderstorm.

For though we be Jamaicans,
maybe love searched and made the guess of a lifetime
and saw where I'd make my beeline to be there in time,
or maybe Love quit job and career, bought plane tickets
and stayed up all night to perhaps see me coming home
like passengers seeing loved ones come in from their flights.
Maybe Love's pointing now and is standing with eyes closed,
arms and smiles wide, preparing for one more embrace.
If raindrops had SMS and GPS, the never could be,
could be favorable and unneverable.
(abrupt stop)

Nevertheless, I'm praying as though gods
exist and life's not fixed,
that my new body and its kiss are strong enough
to stay, more than the pain of the stain because I'm missed.
I'm searching through lightning's celebrity appearances and thunder's envy.
Trying to make it home, home to you; home is you.
Close falls and near landings,
raindrops who freefall with no license and recklessness,
hinder all possibilities of coming to you.

I miss you. I'm sorry I'm no longer there for you,
but I've relived every memory I saved of you
before this forty-five-thousandth six hundredth
and seventy-seventh attempt; I fall and see all the images of you
in the raindrops around me; it was as if you were the rain
and I was a part of your make up.
Don't you sense me, dear?
As feet in freefall are to be compared to my heart beat, love?
Is hope too dear for love?

Are you still hurt, Love?
I know we used to wish upon a star,
but I would wish upon every tear and every staggered breath
until the afterlife has been used so many times
that it's on the brink of death.
I'll try and retry to see the afterlife,
would it be selfish if I asked you to meet the afterlife.
(abrupt stop)

I'm still falling in death even
after never falling while alive. Do you see me, love?
Why aren't you here to catch me as I fall?
I need you, love, to exist and to be.
When will you, would you please, if you could,
salvage any memory of me?
I need you in the rain;
I could never stomach seeing you in the cemetery.
I'm sorry, but I had to leave
for you and our Love to be free as can be.
I wish for you to love again, only if you come to be with me.

I fall, surrounded by the hopelessness of despair as winds...
(abrupt stop)

How many afterlives will I relive
'til you realise that we lived the best
we could with our mortal lives;
struggling to love on each other
'til our affections were immortalised
disappointment took your reason to live
well I'm here to prove there's more to life
and if you believe you'll see love in all its glory
if you look beyond the pain of your mortal...

(abrupt stop)

Somewhere over the Himalayas where the sunrise
isn't as beautiful compared to waking up to you—
because if raindrops were the tears of loved ones past,
then every hurricane that ever came
was showers of love or water asteroids of pain.

We fell, falling separately,
some for adrenaline, the rest plunging desperately
with hope or revenge on our minds;
jumping into the skies
as though equipped with parachutes from heaven,
every second of our nosedive
before we fail our mission and elsewhere collide—
reincarnation gets us back up
like a kid on his favorite ride.

(abrupt stop)

I see love, running into the ocean
as I am about to crash in
fighting to live as myself, and other water comets come crashing
I see love, and as always my body begins to shake
landing somewhere near the Indian ocean.
Who knew the gods would have us see each other
in our favorite place?
Love sees me, as my being begins to disintegrate
Love, have you come to save me?
I tried, but this time might be the last
As the gods would have it that you meet Fate.
just to see you again was all I needed
Is there hope for us to touch? Or is it too late?

The Misappropriation of Now: Part III

It's sorta crazy to me, we are unprepared for the future and now show it,
while we are ill-prepared now and the future will show it.
Now is the only currency we don't work for, that is inherently invaluable,
but worthless if never invested properly (I like that, invest in your now).
We spend time, money and sacrifice so much for places we want to go or be,
so much effort for something not yet seen or experienced.
We should always be prepared for now, simply because we're always there;
now is like life in slow motion, well maybe it's actually life in normal speed.
See, now gives us the perspective of the whole picture,
because looking and moving in the future takes away the details—
they get lost in the eagerness, the possibility and the hopes.
Our nows need us for the future; maybe they even need us in spite of it.
Your now needs more attention, more practice for your future ones;
better yet create a now that'll forever illuminate your future nows.

'TIL OCEANS THIRST

I'm drowning, in a cacophony of clichés
tossed by the current... heartbreaks and replays.
Deeper- yet deeper still, a dire thrill as
each wave sends me tumbling into its dark night;
a cruel sight as I flail in fright-crumbling inside
while this ocean of loneliness has its way with me and away with me.
I'm barely alive, avoiding the light
and hope is hopeless in hopes of a love life being revived.
Woe is me, swimming against a school of impossibilities
and as far as I can see- this might be the ending scene
as my end is seen, destiny brought me here
I lament this watery finale;
but I'm fighting till death, for a breath to breathe,
wrestling for dear life from deaths reprieve.

Air is what I lack, but love is my greatest need
one in the same, I'm drowning in pain
heart and brain suffocates and asphyxiates.
Failure tickles as I collide, my World's in sight
and to love again my life's a lowly sacrifice.
Desperations made me brave
though my attempts crash against the waves.
Breast stroke, back stroke -
whichever manoeuvre will get me near,
stroke for life versus stroke of death
without the touch of love I fear.

Determined against whatever odds to reverse my fate,
return to sender looms as I traverse with waves.
Breathe- don't breathe- this sea flips me recklessly
as it surfs towards victory.
I am exhausted- yet still love falls and I just flail
faint of heart unable to regenerate.
She's closer to this end- and I'm closer to mine
swimming as I cry, tears and fears
drown in the oceans laughter
completely worried I won't make it in time.
And here now, where no coincidences exist,
transfixed amidst, a myriad of conflicts,
my determination still persists.

I will not die here, not before love as she did me
I will live, even if I have to kill the sea
I will not beg nor will I seek mercy from you, oh mere sea!
One of us will soon meet their mortality!
Indubitable inevitability!
My cause is greater than your thrill for execution!
I will make your abode the headstone of destitution!

How can you murder love
as it blazes a trail across your waves!
You cannot- not now and not today!
When have you ever been overwhelmed by all your senses?
Have you experienced passions reignited as love
bombards barriers and breaks down defences?
Who have you loved even if death is the only way to show it.

Tears fall, and so does she
the ocean churns, as jealousy spurns
I still swim desperately as love is falling and falling more rapidly!
Oh Sea, who has loved you, as I love her?
Distress has only made my passion worst
I'm praying again since the last time, this is the first.
I'm praying my affections are enough to make oceans thirst!
A fire ignites, and hope incites;
I promise to catch you if you fall
a promise to keep and a reason to fight.
This feeling is for the first time is so surreal
I'd live one more moment just to die with you.
I'm dying for air, while dying for love
and she's diving through air, just to die in love.

This ocean will not kill me,
you will never hinder our love, nor our reunion
to live for death is my viable solution!
I will love you 'til the ocean begins to thirst
'til the mechanics of the sea ceases to work!
Love can do the impossible
it can make seas part and oceans parched!
Suffocating for love is temporary
when suffocating from love is its remedy.
I'll love, more than breathing- even if death is the prize
I'll love you desperately 'til this sea is filled with jealousy
and brings insecurities in its tides.

Love is near, and I am here overwhelmed by this sudden rush,
just to live for one more touch.
The moments come -it now seems like I am done
I can't believe- here we are again
this time united in love for an eternity.

WE TOUCH
and just then- as love rekindles,
so does the revenge of the ocean
and then I remember- how could I forget,
as I scream out "Eouxheun!!!"
Conflicted- as I attempt to savour love touching me
our souls kissed
a second of distraction means a moment was missed.

My whole world- now a wet spot among others
I can't recall where specifically
but here's my outcome- outworked and undone.
Drunk by the sea, as she drank efforts and mortality.
Physically lifeless- all my energy worn,
I met love, now I'm loveless as love left me torn.
At the mercy of the seas
lost in the ocean and a loss to Eouxheun.
I'm so sorry baby girl, if only you could hear me,
this is all so confusing.
Dear, life is yours to make of it
you will have it and you will lose it
make a habit of it for your choosing.
I couldn't live without your mother
and I know this isn't soothing
but baby girl its ok- daddy went to -
better yet daddy went too
daddy loves you very much-
but right now he's snoozing.

Eouxheun's Prayer: Undo

Who will teach me to love like you?
To trust despite utter despair?
Who will love me if not you two?
Mommy's snoozing, daddy sleeping:
can any one of you hear?

Who will tell me it's okay
"when it ain't; I'm sorry, dad–when it's not"?
Who will bake while I run my fingers
around the edges of the muffin pots?

Is whoever you prayed to
readily available to undo
the events that make me miserable?
Can we perchance rewind
or turn back
the already turned backhands of time?

If you're listening, please rescind
all the calamities that led to the unregrettable
tragedies and incontrovertible catastrophes.

Undo the unsaid I love yous
and emotions we hung up in our mental closets,
take back the heartbreaks and the egos
that caused it.

Undo it all. Undo it all.

Bring back mommy from the incurable sleeps
resuscitate the soul of daddy and bring him back to me.
Please, both of you just breathe.
Come back if only to tell me you love me
Undo the consequences of their stain,
undo all the attempts to hide the pain!

Take it back,

the grudges that were foundations
for the towering skyscrapers of regret!
Take it back through the canal of Forget,
where Love resets and the sun rises
from the water cemetery where their passion rests.
Undo it all and set me free,
undo whatever that needs be.
You died for love, such a romantic novelty
the emblem of selfishness and cruelty
is this how it was supposed to go?

After the sacrifices, whose love am I shown?

Alone with only these painful memories
contemplating existential mysteries;
maybe, just maybe
since my parents loved each other
'til their last breath
maybe, just maybe
the sea will love me to death.
Please both of you just breathe!
(silence)
Well, here's my final walk as I inch closer to eternity,
the final piece of the trinity.
Now we're all together, a loving family
sleeping and snoozing peacefully...

THE CONCLUSION

Finis Capitis

Truth is, I wasnt good at closings or endings.
I was usually the person waiting on the end in utmost discomfort
until it dies away into my freedom. I used to get anxious and annoyed
when it came to the end. With the closing of this chapter, I found it
emotionally anxietous to finish. I welled up with screamingly silent cries,
and at the same time visibly overcome with tears. This wasn't just an end
to a book, it was the end of unrelenting taxes and bouts of pain,
the harvests of misery, unrealistic demands of broken love, pointless ideals,
crippling loyalties and googolous other events that subheaded
the experiences I had gone through. I became overwhelmed and clueless;
still allowed my being to calculate the requirements for the task
that had to be completed. I still don't know how to, but this will be my attempt.

:Leaves self:

Akiim, my dear self,
Look at what you've been able to accomplish!
No matter the time it took, look at the work you've been able to eke out,
despite the losses, the deaths, the depression, the thoughts of suicide-
not to mention the heartbreaks, the disappointments,
the lessons and any obstacle that greeted you with discomfort.
Just look, see how far you've come! Look where you came from
and be proud of who you are. You aren't the tragedies
that bullied you for years, tattooing misery throughout your being;
that isn't who you are and it is a false narrative of who you were.
You aren't the unloved little boy you thought you were
because everyone left and no one was around long enough
to appreciate you for you while you tried to circumnavigate
the inner intricacies of your overly complex and complicated being.

Akiim, you weren't always the best of everything,
but when you were bad you were awful through and through,
but be grateful that the person and being that you were-
you no longer are and that version of you is unreturnable.
The maladious miseries that defined your worldview
for so long isn't here and that is why this book was necessary.
It wasn't just for the creative aesthetic, it was for the healing of your being-
truth is you are a beautiful yet dark soul, and your healing comes
in the process and speaks volumes in your writings.
Cease from being so doubtful of your power,
cease from being so muted and tame
because of the transient beings you hold in high regard.
Be the fullness of your darkness and the pinnacle of your beauty,
choosing to be all of your destinuous self regardless of the situation or context.
Rise from the depths of the deep 'til the deep is as shallow
as the expanse of the universe. Rise Akiim, rise-
from the dreariness of of your past and pain you've memorised.

You've conquered this era,
you've mastered this time period in its fullness,
and even now a new chapter looms- just look how accomplished
you've become in the old chapters and breathe every sigh of relief
that you aren't alone and will be supremely protected, loved and blessed.
Be proud of yourself Akiim, Fortune and Destiny have found favour in you
and have chosen to adorn you thusly. It comes at a cost,
and the process is the process, but don't forget
that the harvest IS THE HARVEST.
The Heartbreak Masterpiece: A Razed Utopia is finished!
Celebrate this feat, celebrate this accomplishment
for it truly is worth celebrating.
You are the greatest adventure you will ever know,
the maestro of your happiness wherever you may go.
You are the greatest adventure you will ever know,
so chart the waters boldly and wisely wherever you may go.
Remember to be kind to yourself in all things,
and be true to the monsters and heroes that wrestle within.
I love you Akiim, always- in all ways.

::returns::

Deep sigh

THE SHIPMAKER

The tempest rages ferociously as it dissuades all who dare look upon her.
She disconcerts all ego from beginning their journey, ridiculing
and taunting daredevils into second guessing if they, by her standards,
are seaworthy. With unending rolls of thunder, Mother Nature proves
to be a merciless sky tactician as she stabs it with relentless coruscations.
The view is threatening, and the reality is uncertain; but the truth
is hidden between the fear to go on and the will to be brave.
I saw this paralyzing spectacle, and it was as though I caught a glimpse
of my own failure to not reach anywhere. I was honestly fazed–truly,
completely daunted; and true to form, when I became overwhelmed,
I retreated... a cycle repeated many times over. Regardless of the increasing
failures to even try, I never failed to dream that I was surfing my way through
the frightening tempest and its glaring dangers.
Truthfully, I was scared of being rejected, deemed not worthy
or not being enough and not being deemed good enough to be good enough
by those who also met the same standard but had a golden wand of approval
which made everyone thirsty for their touch.
I just couldn't see the horizon, and it scared me.
How do I give my all to something I couldn't see the end of?
How do I know if it'd pay off? I was super nervous, I was sure of my footing
on the seashore, but not so confident with the heavy armour of insecurity.
I kept dreaming I'd conquer it, but I didn't know if there was a how
or even a when. And no matter how much I didn't know,
I was certain that I wanted to. Like I wanted to... like for real I wanted to.
I just needed a boat maker and the right boat: for me the boat maker
has to be omniscient about weather, one who was also adeptly knowledgeable
about the intricacies of my idiosyncrasies and the right boat
someone like me would need. Since I knew I couldn't do
it on my own, no matter how much I tried, I knew I wasn't enough.
Because truth is, if we feel secure with the ship; we can sleep eat
and enjoy ourselves regardless of the impending weather;
and in front of me was clearly the greatest boat I could ever imagine or ever need.
And for that, I thank the ShipMaker and the Ship for helping cross many
a raging sea safely. Truth is, the right ship gets you across turbulent seas
and tumultuous weather. It helps with the doubts of what could be,
when they aren't. It affords a chance when you don't give yourself one.
A good ship supports before there is a need for it, because that's what it was built for.
A good ship provides safety because the ShipMaker took into account
the kind of weather it would be used for. A good ship affords hope,
it affords peace and is the silver lining throughout the entirety of the journey.
The ShipMaker, of course, is the Creator, and the ship made up of the amazing friends
and loved ones who supported me while I struggled to persevere countless times over.
I went through inspirational highs even plummeted and wallowed through
the misery of undetectable lows, and still they sailed on, with and without wind;
and for you, I am grateful, immensely, completely and eternally.

Thank you and from all of me
LoveAndLoyaltyUndeniableUnquestioned

The Perfect Expressive Manifestation of Cerebral Expression

Conducting Alqhumy with The Alqhumizt ChlokWirk (ChL)

Legendary Greatness Arranged by:

Akiim Aeiat

Writing's Sacrosanct Virtuoso
The Qhuillustrious High Emperor
of Alqhumetria,
First Fifthian and Pensiah,
Teyhguwehtel

The Fell Types
Are Digitally Reproduced
by Igino Marini
www.iginimarini.com

Cover Illustration
done by:
Bryan Ward
HouseBryanWard@gmail.com
instagram: housebryanward

Akiim Aeiat
979-8-9855453-8-8 (hardcover)
979-8-9855453-4-0 (paperbook)
Published by Grammerlin Square
www.grammerlinsquare.com
grammerlinsq@gmail.com

Printed in Poland
by Amazon Fulfillment
Poland Sp. z o.o., Wrocław
26 July 2022

bf38d311-2781-4439-a9a9-6f95adc99d45R01